MW01700730

THE HEAVENLY MAN

With the compliments of

DR. JOHN W. LUCAS

President

"The Maranatha Evangelistic Association"

P.O. Box 1292, Calgary, Alberta T2P 2L2

Phone: (403) 283-2263 Fax: 283-4061

E-mail: lucasjw@cadvision.com

Engaged in a co-operative voluntary partnership with

"ASIALINK"

"Asian Outreach Canada"

and the

"Back To Jerusalem Movement" *in China*

The Heavenly Man

Guardian
BOOKS

Belleville, Ontario, Canada

THE HEAVENLY MAN

ISBN: 1-55306-160-8

For more information or to order additional copies, please contact:

Dale Hiscock
c/o Asian Outreach Canada
P.O. Box 939, Cambridge, ON N1R 5X9
(519) 624-0223
E-mail: aocan@golden.net

Printed in Canada
by
Guardian BOOKS

Table of Contents

Preface

North America Edition

Håvald Slåatten of Norway has given outstanding service to the English speaking world in writing this soul-stirring account of God's faithfulness in the life of "The Heavenly Man."

Asian Outreach Canada (asialink canada) Executive Director, the Rev. Dale R. Hiscock and his wife, Delreen, along with the assistance of Gord and Margaret Jones are to be commended for such dedicated editing of the original manuscript prior to publishing this North American edition.

This project would not have been possible without the dedicated and amazing effort of Sigbjorn Killerud (translator), Rune Aasen, our graphic artist and the tremendous support of our Asialink Network partner in Norway and it's Director, Toby Killerud.

Pastor Yun's vivid testimony is a faith stimulant for life's seemingly impossible situations. My personal acquaintanceship with this contemporary "hero of faith" has been a spiritually enriching experience. The privilege of praying with "The Heavenly Man" was a never to be forgotten moment. He is so eternally minded and such a Godly intercessor. Fervent in prayer, he believes for the spiritual well being of his countrymen and that "Sinim" (China, see Isaiah 49:10 KJV) shall be saved.

Prayerfully read this exciting narrative. Circulate it widely amongst your friends and associates. Increase your missionary vision!

We are living in an era of prophetic fulfillment!

"For the earth will be full of the knowledge of the Lord as the waters cover the sea." (Isaiah 11:9b NIV)

Dr. John W. Lucas
Immanuel Assembly
Calgary, Alberta, Canada
September, 2000

Introduction

Missionaries from the western world sailed for China more than a hundred years ago. They met resistance from the locals, struggled with deplorably inadequate living conditions, fervently endeavored to master another language, suffered for their faith and many paid the supreme price with their life.

As they sowed in tears, they didn't realize that a tremendous gathering of precious souls would enter God's Kingdom many years later. Today, China's revival is considered the greatest spiritual harvest since the book of Acts. China's Christians are reaping a rich spiritual harvest with shouts of joy. (Psalm 126:5-6)

Some western mission leaders look for the prospect of an open door into China so that western missionaries can return for ministry in that great nation. I believe that opportunity is past.

The new millennium has ushered in dramatic changes. National missionaries are preparing to pour out of China to other nations. Thousands have received a Divine calling from God to leave China and evangelize the world. They are ready to go having been purified and tempered through the fires of fiery persecution and political resistance. This is not something new—for almost 100 years God has been preparing the Chinese Church for such an hour as this. They have a Heavenly call to take the Gospel to the Buddhist, Hinduistic and Islamic areas of the world.

"The Heavenly Man" is at the forefront of this missionary emphasis. A second generation Christian, his Mother was converted to Christianity through the witness of a Norwegian missionary. He visits the western world to give thanks for the dedication of those pioneer missionaries who planted the seed. He challenges contemporary Christians to stand together with their Chinese brothers and sisters in world evangelization. The task is to bring the Gospel "Back to Jerusalem", as they so aptly put it, through the most unevangelized regions of the world.

This book will challenge, inspire and could emotionally disturb you when reading about the torturous persecution endured by the contemporary Church in China.

May you be motivated to stand together and support our fellow Chinese believers in their gigantic task of bringing the Gospel "back to (their) Jerusalem."

Dale R. Hiscock
Executive Director, Asian Outreach Canada
Part of the Asialink Network
"Making A Difference That Lasts"

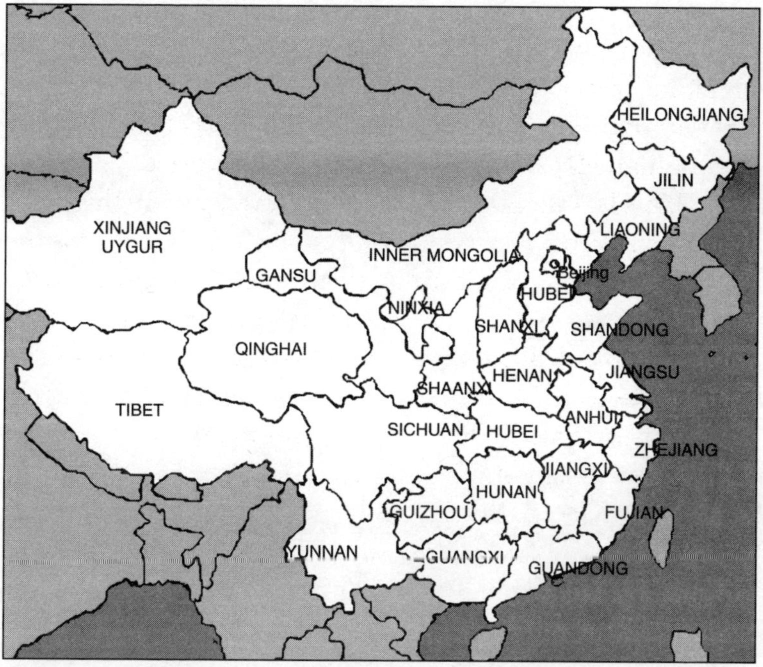
HEILONGJIANG
JILIN
LIAONING
XINJIANG
UYGUR
INNER MONGOLIA
GANSU
Beijing
HUBEI
NINXIA
SHANXI
SHANDONG
QINGHAI
HENAN
JIANGSU
TIBET
SHAANXI
ANHUI
SICHUAN
HUBEI
ZHEJIANG
JIANGXI
HUNAN
GUIZHOU
FUJIAN
YUNNAN
GUANGXI
GUANDONG

Chapter One

"Go to the West and Go to the South"

For nearly a decade, the Cultural Revolution's unpredictable Red Guard, unleashed by Chairman Mao Tse-tung, created great havoc throughout China. Economic and political chaos prevailed in all aspects of society. The people lived in anguish, with little to eat, never knowing what would happen next. However, they had become used to this, both before and after Chairman Mao came to power in 1949. Floods, drought and especially power struggles, from gangs, landowners and revolutionary cadres, were all too common. The Chinese people had lived through centuries of upheaval.

It was 10 o'clock one evening in 1975, and most of the inhabitants in this little Chinese town in central China had retired for the evening. They, like most people in China at this time, had endured a long exhausting day of hard physical labour, and they looked forward to the evening and finally a time of rest.

Seventeen-year-old Yun had also gone to bed. He had prayed a long time, as usual, before retiring for the night. He spent much time praying and reading his Bible, this costly gift which he had received some time ago. He was one of a few in the area who had a Bible, and the way in which he received it had created great wonder among the Christians. This was such a dear book to him. The whole day long he had it with him, at work and at home. And he took it with him to bed every night laying it on his chest. Yun not only read the Bible—he memorized vast portions of it, like the Gospel according to Matthew and the book of Acts. He anxiously waited for God to send him out to be a witness for Jesus Christ.

That night, Yun had just laid his head on the pillow, when suddenly he sat up and jumped out of his bed. He rushed to his parents who had not yet fallen asleep, and asked his mother, "Did you call me? Is there anything you want me for?"

His mother responded, "No, why?"

Astonished, Yun replied, "But then, who was calling me and shouting out my name? And who touched me?" His mother—as much in wonder as Yun was—replied that neither she nor Yun's father had said anything to him. "No one has called you, just go back to bed and go to sleep," she commanded.

Half an hour later, he heard the voice again. It was very distinct this time. "Brother Yun! You must go to the west and then to the south and preach the Gospel! You shall be my witness."

And once again, he went to his mother to tell her what he had heard. She became frightened and feared that her son's imagination was out of control. He went back to bed, kneeled down again and prayed: "Lord, if this is You who is calling me, tell me what You want. I am willing to be Your witness."

Later that morning, at around 4 a.m. Yun had a vision. He saw an old man whom he had seen in a dream previously. It was at this time that he had received his prized Bible in the vision (and as you will read in chapter 3, this later became a reality). Now the old man came near to him, and repeated the words Yun himself had heard earlier that evening. "You shall go first to the west, and then to the south. You shall preach the Gospel and be my witness."

Then the vision changed, and suddenly Yun saw a huge gathering of people. The old man, who radiated great authority, asked him to testify before this large assembly. Yun hesitated for a moment. The old man then asked him to pray for a demon possessed woman who was in the crowd. Obediently, he began to pray. The women struggled as if she were in the throes of death. After much prayer she was completely set free from the demonic spirit that had controlled her.

Everyone who saw this was totally astonished. A young man who was in the crowd of onlookers came to him and asked if he was Brother Yun. He explained that the brothers and sisters in his village had fasted and prayed three days for Yun to come and preach to them.

Yun asked where the young man came from. "I come from the south." Then he gave Yun his name and the name of his village. Yun was deeply touched by this man's sincerity and promised to come the next day.

When Yun awoke from his vision he was now certain that God had called him to preach the Gospel—both in the west and in the south.

Chapter Two

Come Home—Jesus Loves You

Yun (not his real name) is from Henan province, an area in the central part of China. Many Norwegian missionaries ministered there before the Second World War, and up to 1950. They left a deep spiritual impression all over this area, with many Chinese people coming to know Jesus Christ as their Saviour.

Compared to other areas in China, there were many Christians in Yun's home area and Yun's mother was one of them. In the 1940s a Norwegian missionary had led her to believe in Christ. But when the communists took control of the country in 1949, most of the Chinese Christian leaders were arrested and sentenced to many years in prison or labour camps. Many were killed.

Of all the religions to be found in China at this time, the one most opposed was Christianity. It was viewed as a western religion that had been imposed from the west upon the Chinese people. It's messengers, the missionaries, were viewed as agents of western imperialism and colonization which the new China wanted no part of. With such drastic changes taking place, the Chinese believers were driven underground, unable to enjoy the fellowship of other believers and the teaching of God's Word. It was obviously dangerous to show that you believed in Jesus Christ.

Yun's mother did not renounce Christ, but due to a variety of reasons her relationship with God grew cold. This was something that happened to many other Chinese believers as well.

Yun was born in 1958, less than 10 years after the communists under Chairman Mao Tse-tung founded the People's Republic. The year 1958 was also the start of a very difficult period for the Chinese. Mao initiated one of his many great experiments to modernize China. He called it "The Great Leap Forward".

Eccentric ideas were released into everyday life. Peasants were encouraged to purchase their own melting-ovens to produce iron and steel for China's growing and needy economy. This and other initiatives were total failures. The iron, which was produced in these primitive melting-ovens, was unfit for use. Tens of millions of the Chinese people wasted valuable working hours to produce an inferior product that was of no value.

The "Great Leap Forward" became a gigantic step backward. The autocratic government under Mao demanded great sacrifice from it's people. Sadly, the people who were to have been liberated by communism were now the very ones paying the price for their leaderships' dream of a utopian state.

The "Great Leap Forward" led to an extensive famine all over China. Yun remembered, as a little boy, begging for food. It was not unusual to see people in Henan, eating grass and bark from the trees to survive. During Yun's first four years of life, approximately eight million people starved to death in Henan province.

When Yun had reached the age of eight, Mao initiated another bold experiment—"The Cultural Revolution". Mao's little red book symbolized the desire of the Chinese to be liberated from all the vices of society, old ideas, old culture, old customs and old habits. Millions of young people, known as the Red Guard, were unleashed to liberate the people. Instead, more torment occurred. Schools and universities were closed, and Yun's young life was touched again. He only received three years of schooling. The Cultural Revolution meant an even harder persecution of the Christians. All churches were closed, and Christians were forbidden to gather for prayer and fellowship. All "superstitious activity", which included Christianity, was to be fought against even more ruthlessly than before. During this time of severe upheaval the Christians were forced to meet secretly. Many new converts were added to the Church.

In 1974 Yun's father became seriously ill. He had a type of asthma which developed into lung cancer, and the illness spread further to his stomach. The doctors had given up all hope for him. This kind of cancer could only lead one way—to death. But old superstitions still existed among the people in the area, and his father asked the village witch doctor to cast the evil spirit of cancer out of him. Yun's father, who believed in the power of the witch doctor, had been encouraging his son to become a disciple of this witch doctor so that he too could become powerful.

Traditionally in China, Yun, like most young men, was ready to obey his father's wishes. For over 2000 years, Confucianism had infiltrated the mindset of the Chinese people, teaching them to be obedient to their parents and the authorities in society. Sixteen-year-old Yun was prepared to learn the art of witchcraft.

His father's illness was difficult for all the members of his family. In addition to not having enough food, they didn't have any money. His mother had already sold much of their belongings to buy medicine. She knew she was about to become a widow. Her thoughts were plagued by fear, wondering how her family would survive without her husband.

One night, as she lay in bed twisted in anguish, unable to sleep, she heard a distinct voice calling her, "Come home. Jesus still loves you!" Sensing something in her heart that she had not felt for so long, she knelt down and prayed to Jesus, asking for forgiveness like a lost daughter who had returned home. The next day she told her family what she had experienced, and then persuaded them to join her in praying to Jesus.

In this way she led her entire family into a relationship with Jesus Christ. As a teenager Yun quickly discovered that the Gospel is much more than words and theory, but it is a supernatural living power able to break spiritual bondages. As a family, they prayed for Yun's father, that he must be healed, and it happened! Within a very short time his father recovered, and was totally healed. It was Yun's first encounter with the power of the Gospel.

Chapter Three

Praying for the Impossible... A Bible

After Yun's family had become Christians they discovered God's peace and joy replacing their worries and despair. Still, Yun was impatient. He felt he owed Jesus so much, and he longed to tell others about God's mercy. But who was this Jesus who had changed their family?

During conversations with his mother she had explained everything that she could remember about Jesus. She retold the story of God's amazing love for mankind in sending His son Jesus, to die on a cross for men's sins. Apparently a book called the Bible contained all His teachings. Her memory of the Bible's teachings was limited yet she passed on the little nuggets of truth that she could recall.

Yun often wondered how he would be able to read about something in a book that he could not get a hold of. He was determined to find the words of Jesus. Scarcely any of the Christians in the area had ever seen a Bible. If you were caught with one during the Cultural Revolution, the police and Red Guard would make your life quite difficult. It was not uncommon to be beaten, kicked, ridiculed, and denounced by your peers. The ultimate price for many was torture and death. As a result, many become secret believers.

The only Bible that existed for those in Yun's village were Bible verses handwritten on small fragments of paper. This was the way the Chinese Christians secretly shared God's Word with each other. Yun was determined to satisfy his longing for a Bible. To actually hold and read this book called a Bible, the Word of God would take a miracle!

To help satisfy her son's deepest desire to see and read a Bible, Yun's mother took him to visit a preacher she knew. She also knew he secretly had a Bible. During their visit the preacher did not show them his Bible, causing Yun and mother to have all kinds of questions. Maybe the preacher just wanted to be careful, or perhaps he thought Yun was too young to understand the value the Word of God. The preacher concluded their visit by encouraging Yun to pray and ask God to give him what he longed for—a Bible. He also suggested that Yun should fast and pray.

"The Bible is the Word of God. It is a book from Heaven. Only by praying to God, can you get it," the man told him. Yun did not understand what fasting meant, so the preacher explained what he should do. He encouraged Yun by saying, "God is faithful. He will reveal Himself to everyone who is looking for Him."

Yun was very poor and did not own anything. He could have asked for many things that he and the family needed, like more food for one. Yet, his desire for a Bible overshadowed everything else. During the next two months, day and night, he prayed and asked God, "Oh, Lord! Give me a Bible, please give me a Bible! Amen." As he continued fasting and praying it seemed that God was not interested in answering his prayers.

He visited the preacher again and told him that he had prayed for a long time, but God didn't answer his prayers. The preacher's response challenged Yun to continue praying and fasting. On returning home Yun prayed even more earnestly for a Bible.

Three months later, one morning while praying, Yun had a vision. In his vision he saw an old man pulling a cart with two younger men helping him (this was the old man we described in the beginning of this story, where he asked Yun to go to the west and to the south). When the old man was still far off, he was filled with compassion towards Yun. As he came alongside Yun, he asked him if he had anything to eat.

Yun was very hungry because his family had no money, and nearly no food. He cried out to the old man that he had nothing to eat. The kindly old man then took a loaf of bread from his cart and gave it to his two helpers. They then passed the bread to Yun. When he began to eat the bread, it suddenly changed into a Bible. He gave thanks with all his heart, "Thank you God! Praise be to Your Name. You heard my prayers and gave me this Bible. I promise to serve You for the rest of my life!"

Early in the morning when Yun awoke, he was so greatly disappointed when he realized it was just a dream. He had no Bible. His parents, who were disturbed by his shouting and talking in his sleep, saw him searching the house looking for something. Had their son gone mad?

His father, deeply concerned that his son was going insane, embraced him and with tears cried out to God. He prayed, "Lord give me back my cancer if that would save my son from going mad. Have mercy on him and give him a Bible." Yun's mother prayed for the same thing. "Pray and you shall get, seek and you shall find."

Suddenly, a knock was heard at the front door, and a voice called out Yun's name. When he opened the door, two men, looking exactly like the men in his dream, stood there. One of them carried a bag, and Yun asked if they had come to give him bread. They answered yes, and Yun asked again, "I mean, did you come to bring me a Bible?"

"Yes, we did, that is, the Holy Bible," they said, and then they gave him a Bible!

The two men were Brother Wang and Brother Song who had traveled from a distant village. They told Yun that during his time of prayer, an evangelist was prompted by the Holy Spirit to give Yun his Bible. The two brothers, who came with the book, were his messengers. In this remarkable way Yun received what he had desperately prayed for, a Bible.

After this incident, Yun had complete confidence in prayer. He avidly read, memorized and meditated on God's Word. It was as if God had written every single word just for him. Once, after reading a verse in Acts, he stopped to allow it to sink into his heart. "But you will receive power when the Holy Spirit comes on you; and you will be my witnesses in Jerusalem, and in all Judea and Samaria, and to the ends of the earth."

"The Holy Spirit, who was that?" When he asked his mother, she struggled to explain what she thought the Holy Spirit was. Her response only confused her son. Yun finally began to pray asking God to give him the Holy Spirit like this verse talked about. "Dear Jesus. I need the Holy Spirit. Please give me Your power. I am willing to be Your witness," he prayed.

Suddenly, something happened. An inexplicable love and revelation of God's presence flooded his being. Songs he had never learned flowed out of him like a raging river. Even today these songs are sung throughout the house churches of China.

These were some of the pivotal moments in Yun's young life as a new Christian, before God called him as an evangelist. Let us continue now from the events in the first chapter, where he received his calling to travel to the west and to the south in his first missions outreach.

Chapter Four

The First Trip West and South

After God spoke into his life, Yun shared with his parents that God had called him to be a witness for Jesus throughout China. His mother wanted to know where God was sending him, but all Yun could tell her was that God had called him to go to the west and then to the south to preach the Gospel.

Yun told his parents of a dream he had received. He explained to them, that after he leaves for the west, a young man will come to their home later that same day. Yun described that the young man would come from the south, wearing a white shirt, gray trousers with patches on the knees.

"When he arrives, you must ask him to wait for me until I return," Yun told his mother. "The people in his village have been praying and fasting for three days that I would come to witness and preach the Gospel to them. The man's name will be Jing Cai Yu." Sensing that God was leading her son, she promptly prayed for his protection even though she did not totally understand what he was talking about.

As Yun left for the west, he was uncertain as to which village he was to go to, so he simply kept walking. He crossed a river, where he met a man who called himself Brother Young. He asked Yun where he was going. Yun replied that God had called him to go to the west and then to the south, to be a witness and preach the Gospel.

When Brother Young heard Yun's story, he was greatly affected and stated, "I have come to meet you, and bring you to my village, which is called West High Village. The brothers and sisters heard how you prayed for a long time to get a Bible, and how God answered your prayers. They are now asking you to come and preach and read to them from your Bible."

When Yun arrived in the village, it was harvest time. As the farmers out in the fields heard about Yun's arrival, they dropped their farming tools and rushed to the home where Yun was staying. They wanted to see his Bible and hear him speak. Children, teenagers, elderly men and women all came running, they had never seen a whole Bible before. When Yun saw their hunger for the Word of God he began to sing the songs the Holy Spirit had given him. Tears flowed down their cheeks as they listened. They eagerly asked for the words to the songs that he had sung and pleaded for him to read from his Bible.

In picking up his Bible, he explained how he had fasted and prayed for days until God answered his prayer. Not knowing how to preach, he began to quote the entire Gospel according to Matthew by memory, from the beginning to the end! Chapter after chapter flowed out from him. The teenager could hardly understand what he said, and the audience understood no more than he did. But the Spirit of God had taken over, and the Word of God was effective. Their hearts were touched by God's love and the truth in what Yun said.

When he had finished quoting the book of Matthew, all 28 chapters, he stood up as if it were time for him to leave the village. But, they wanted more! So, he then continued by quoting from the book of Acts. The first twelve chapters flowed from him.

When Yun had first arrived in the village, there were only a few Christians, yet by the time he left the number of believers had increased dramatically. This was Yun's first time to speak about the kingdom of God. He was only 16 years of age.

He shared with the villagers that he had to go to the south, where there were others expecting him. A woman asked him what village he had to travel to. Yun responded that he was to meet a man, and he told her his name. With a surprised look the woman asked, "Do you know this man?" Yes, he did in a way. He had met him earlier in the morning, in his dream, where he had promised to come to the village to witness and preach. The sister fell silent for a moment as tears filled her eyes, "He's my brother," she replied.

This woman had grown up in this village that Yun was on his way to. She had witnessed about Jesus there, and many had received Him as their Savior. She had also told the villagers how Yun had received his Bible. In the village there were many who were fasting and praying for Yun to come and preach.

As Yun began his journey back home, a miracle took place, just as it had for Philip in the book of Acts. Yun lived about two walking hours from the village he had traveled to in the west. As he started on his journey, suddenly, without any time passing, he was at home in his village by his parent's house.

When he came inside the house, his mother was so happy to see him. "Just after you left, the man you said would come, came, and he looked exactly the way you described him. I asked him if his name was Yu, and if he came from the south. He was quite surprised, because everything that I told him was right. I asked him if he and the others in his village had fasted and prayed three days for my son to come and read from the Bible? When he heard this, he was not only surprised—he became frightened. "How on earth did you know all this? We have never met before," he replied. I told him that God had shown all this to my son in a dream. I also told him that you promised to travel to their village later today when you came back."

Yun asked his mother where the man was. "He is not here," his mother said. "I asked him if he wanted some water to drink, but he left right away to tell the other Christians in his village that God had heard their prayers. He was so enthusiastic he even forgot his straw hat."

While Yun talked with his mother, the villager, Yu, returned exhausted from his journey, sweat pouring down his face. Yun took Yu's hands and looked at him. Why, the man looked exactly like he had seen in his dream. Yun said, "You are Brother Yu, and you and the others in your village have been praying three days for me to come. All this I saw in a dream last night. Jesus loves you." Yu embraced him and sobbed. Yun's mother now understood that there was nothing wrong with her son's mental health or his imagination. She then blessed her son and his visitor, and then they departed for the village in the south, just as dusk set in.

This was Yun's first time to travel to the west and to the south, witnessing about Jesus Christ as an evangelist. The fire of the Gospel spread rapidly—with signs and wonders.

As a teenager, Yun's understanding of 'the west and the south' was limited to his village and the surrounding area. Gradually, over the past 25 years, that territory has extended to the whole of China and now it even reaches to countries outside of China.

Every free hour, Yun read the Bible. Though he never attended a bible school, he studied, memorized and meditated on the Word. His later ministry successes were due to his understanding that we must study the Word, and then act in faith, putting it into practice.

"When the Lord has asked me to do something, I have always been willing to obey," he says.

Chapter Five

Persecution, Revival and New Openness

As is always the case, wherever there is revival there will be opposition, persecution and suffering. Yun and his mother, along with many of the other Christians, were arrested, beaten, put in prison, and humiliated on numerous occasions by the Public Security Bureau police (PSB). They were accused of illegally preaching publicly about the Christian faith. Although Satan used all means possible, he was unable to snuff out the fire of revival. During this time of persecution, the revival fires burned brightly in all directions.

A village in the south where Yun had been was visited unexpectedly by the police just days after he was there. The police eagerly arrested all the Christians in the village. Amazingly, the Christians' response to being handcuffed and arrested was a tremendous sense of joy which was released in holy laughter. After all, Brother Yun had shared with them the words of Jesus, that told them to be happy when they were persecuted. The way they expressed their joy was by laughing. The police had never known anyone that laughed when they were arrested. Thinking that the Christians were ridiculing and humiliating them, the police began to beat the Christians.

Over time the security police soon realized that Yun was a key leader to the many Christians in that county. Yun's name began to show up regularly in the police records, first at the local level, then the county level, and then in the province. Eventually his name became well known by the authorities in the neighbouring provinces, as well.

During his first year as a Christian, Yun led several thousand people to Christ. When he was 18 years old, he began traveling to other provinces. As a 20-year-old man, he began to organize teaching schools for his co-workers. He understood the necessities of a thorough education in the Word of God.

At the same time he was connected with the underground house churches of China. One of the largest networks of house churches was called the "Born Again" movement, having their roots in Yun's home area. This is the area where Norwegian missionaries had planted the seed of God's Word for half a century. These missionaries had strongly emphasized that becoming a Christian, meant being born again.

Many of the spiritual leaders for the house churches were young people. It was not the age which mattered, but the spiritual maturity which determined who should be the leaders. In the winter of 1978, Brother Yun and his co-workers started baptizing new believers. They baptized mostly at night, when it could be done with less risk of being caught. In the winter they would baptize new Christians by chopping a hole in the ice on the rivers, and immerse them under the cold water. Hundreds could be baptized during one night.

On September 9, 1976, "the Great Helmsman" of China, Mao Tse-tung died, and with him the Cultural Revolution and its gruesome excesses. The economy of the country was in shambles. Chinese society was out of order. In many ways China had regressed in it's development. The nation had an urgent need for stability and normalized conditions.

In 1979, when Yun was 21 years old, Deng Xiaoping became China's premier leader. Deng immediately put in motion the means to normalize China, which was so needy. As a part of his new "Open Door Policy," he gave some form of religious freedom—at least as much as the Christians had experienced at the beginning of the 1950s.

Deng's new government reestablished what it called five patriotic religious organizations to represent the major religions of Buddhism, Taoism, Islam, Catholicism and Protestantism.

The organization responsible for all Protestant Christians was called the Three Self Patriotic Movement (TSPM or the Three-Self Church). The TSPM was originally established in the 1950s by mainly liberal theologians. During the Cultural Revolution all religious activity including the TSPM were banned. Now under Deng the TSPM was reinstated.

The communist party found it necessary to recognize the religious faith of its people by giving them religious freedom to a limited degree. They believed all religions would soon die. According to Marxist teaching, it was just a question of progress and sufficient education, before all forms of religion were eradicated from the minds of the people.

There was one indispensable condition to this newfound religious freedom—the government must control it. The religious organizations were required not to be in conflict with the government's values and goals for rebuilding Chinese society.

Today's TSPM is assisted by the China Christian Council and the Office of Religious Affairs, which takes care of the political policy of the communist party. Together they make sure that the party's policies, regarding religion, are being implemented in the government controlled churches, either with an 'iron-hand' or a 'silk-glove' approach.

Similar to the situation in the former Eastern Europe, where people lived under the iron heel of communism, the people of China are told that they can freely believe in Jesus, but they must keep it to themselves. All preaching and services are to take place only in those churches registered with the government and only for those 18 years of age and older! Preaching the Gospel in public is strictly forbidden.

On the grassroots level within the registered TSPM Church, there are many Christians who are eager to tell others about their faith, even outside their church buildings. However, they first must obtain governmental approval, before proceeding (to be allowed to preach).

The house church movement has rejected all this, and will not be governed or ruled by others who do not acknowledge God's Word. From their perspective it is totally unacceptable to allow an atheistic government to be the head of the Church! Brother Yun has continually been a spokesman for the independence of the house church movement from governmental control.

Chapter Six

DON'T BE A JUDAS

While Yun was on his very first missions trip to the south, God gave him an unusual song to sing. It was a song about not failing, a warning to the believers not to be a Judas. The song talked about the need for the Chinese church to be a brave and faithful witness for God, not willing to compromise to this world's power and authorities. This was something Yun would soon be tested on.

In April 1979, the government approved the reopening of churches under the control of the TSPM. The ministers, priests and believers, who attended these churches, were registered as members of the "Three-Self Church." Spiritual hunger was enormous and many came rushing to these churches. For the first time in many years they were able to pray and hear the Gospel proclaimed. Many good things were happening. However, those who did not accept the control of the atheist communist government over the Church carried the burden of being associated with the house church movements. All over China these groups grew in numbers and strength.

Until the 1980s, the house churches in China operated independently of each other. As they grew larger and larger, they gradually united under various networks. In this way the house churches connected to each other all over the length and breadth of China. We will return to this later.

Experience shows that in communist countries they often use severe methods to gain control of the underground churches. This was also the case in China. One method commonly used is called the "silk-glove" approach.

Near the end of 1980, the communist party along with the Public Security Bureau arranged a meeting for religious leaders and key people in the area where Yun lived. This was all part of their strategy of reestablishing control of the Chinese churches under the TSPM, a religious organization controlled by the government. At this time of new openness it was difficult to see the politics underneath.

The 120 delegates who attended this meeting represented Christianity, Islam, Buddhism and Taoism. Their purpose in meeting was to elect a council and a chairman for each religion. The government had actually nominated Yun to be the chairman of the council for the Protestant Christians. When the vote was taken, most of the delegates voted for him, with the exception of some liberal theologians and other Christians who had forsaken and abandoned the Church back in the 1950s.

One of the ministers, a Mr. Ho, who had voted against Yun, spoke to the assembly telling them Yun was totally unqualified for this position. He stated Yun was unschooled and had never studied theology. He further accused Yun and the other young evangelists of being false preachers. Ho then continued to describe himself as being a believer ever since he was in his mother's womb, even though he had given up his faith during the Cultural Revolution. He boasted that he had once studied in a missionary school. He continued by telling them that, since freedom of religion was restored again, he was the right person to take care of the affairs of the Church in China for that area.

He pointed at Yun and others—who according to his opinion were occupied with subversive activities—and said they were all false evangelists who practiced detestable acts like casting out demons and healing by prayer. He accused them of confusing the people and disturbing the social order.

The police and the communist party's delegates appreciated this conceited speech. They were delighted to hear this verbal attack from a man who was willing to let himself be used in order to achieve a favourable position in the religious system. Ho was encouraged to come forward with more criticism against Yun and the other evangelists. The police chief stated that the scandals among the Christians were seldom told in public. Now he wanted to hear more, and asked Ho, "Tell us how these phony preachers are disturbing the social order."

Encouraged to speak, Ho's confidence soared as his voice rose louder and louder with accusations against Yun, who kept quiet. Finally, Yun could no longer restrain himself as disparaging statements were made against the house churches, the evangelists, and those leaders who had received a calling from God. The Church of God was being disgraced. Yun struck the table and stood up, shouting, "In the name of the Lord Jesus Christ, I command you to be silent!"

Everyone in the meeting was shocked. What did this young 22-year-old have that was worth saying in such a rude manner to these elderly and educated gentlemen? Did he not owe them respect? Yun, consumed by the Holy Spirit, wasn't finished, "God is displeased with this kind of meeting," he stated. Pointing at Ho he said, "Shame on you for discrediting the Church before unbelievers. The Lord Jesus Christ will judge you! The Scripture tells us, do not be yoked with unbelievers. What kind of fellowship can light have with darkness?"

Some brothers and sisters rushed to Yun and asked him to sit down. Those in charge of the meeting were speechless. They soon recovered their composure though, and one of them smashed his hand on the table. He would have no more of these troublemakers and agitators. He told them to leave immediately. Yun shouted out that he would go and never participate in this again.

He had made his choice, and by that he allowed God to lead him on a path filled with pain and sorrow. Soon after this meeting, the Word of God came to him again. This time it was regarding leaders who think only of themselves and not their church. He wept, as the words from the prophet Ezekiel came to his mind—

"And the word of the Lord came to me: Son of man, prophesy against the shepherds of Israel; prophesy and say to them: This is what the Sovereign LORD says: Woe to the shepherds of Israel who only take care of themselves! Should not shepherds take care of the flocks? You eat the curds, clothe yourselves with the wool and slaughter the choice animals, but you do not take care of the flock. You have not strengthened the weak or healed the sick or bound up the injured. You have not brought back the strays or searched for the lost. You have ruled them harshly and brutally. So they were scattered because there was no shepherd, and when they were scattered they became food for all the wild animals. My sheep wandered over all the mountains and on every high hill. They were scattered over the whole earth, and no one searched or looked for them." (Ezekiel 34:1-6)

Since that time, this scripture has been a cornerstone for Yun's ministry not to establish churches that are controlled by the government or secular authorities. In leaving the meeting that day, Yun felt free as a bird, as if he'd escaped a trap set by the Devil. The words of Jeremiah, were also in his thoughts—

"I appointed you as a prophet to the nations.... Do not say, I am only a child. You must go to everyone I send you and say whatever I command you. Do not be afraid of them, for I am with you and will rescue you, declares the Lord.... Today I have made you a fortified city, an iron pillar and a bronze wall to stand against the whole land—against the kings of Judah, its officials, its priests and the people of the land. They will fight against you but will not overcome you, for I am with you and will rescue you, declares the Lord." (Jeremiah 1:5, 7-8, 18-19)

A huge calling was upon his young life. According to the authorities he was now regarded as an enemy of the people. The police were hunting him constantly. The words which Jesus said before He was taken to Heaven, burned in Yun's heart, "When you are persecuted in one place, flee to another.... And you go preach this message: The Heavenly Kingdom is near.... Heal the sick, raise the dead." (Matthew 10:7, 8, 23)

After the meeting with the authorities, Yun had an even deeper insight about what he and the other top-leaders of the house churches were called to do. God used these insights to help them build a church that was founded and based upon the Word of God and not the communist party.

This meant a life of preaching on the run.

At this time, the Lord gave Yun a unique vision of the Kingdom of God. In it he was instructed to stand and work together with those spiritual warriors who shared the same vision. The Holy Spirit had given him a song, which ends like this; "Wheat and weed grow together. Peter and Judas are both present. Some love the Lord, some betray him. Servants of God, do not hesitate to stand up, and judge sin."

Later the house churches of China made a mutual declaration of their beliefs and goals. In point three of this document, they stated this about the Three-Self Church. "All preachers and other workers in the congregations must realize that the Three-Self Church is not a church, but it is a whore, a political organization which serves the atheistic government. We must not be a part of it, but seek to save those sheep who this church has control over."

Point four of this declaration describes the characteristics of a true congregation. In it, they state that the Body of Christ, the Bride, can only consist of those who are born again. That is, people who realize their situation, that they need to repent, and accept Jesus as Savior and Lord. They must turn from their evil ways, and receive the grace of Christ. The Church is consequently not a building, nor is it an organization, but it is a body, a living organism. The Word of God states that a congregation consists of living stones with Jesus Christ as the cornerstone.

To show their commitment to the Gospel, the leaders of the various house churches in January 2000, reaffirmed that their ministry will not focus on erecting church buildings. Rather, they will use their resources solely for evangelizing and mission work. All this challenges the existing religious system inside China—nearly to the same degree as it would here in the west.

Chapter Seven

ARREST AND FLIGHT

We in the west need to understand that the scathing criticism of the Three-Self Church was not a decision by a few men, but it is the summation of thought and revelation from many of the Chinese believers.

By 1980, Yun had become a leading spokesperson in disclosing the Three-Self Church for what it was. Soon, he would face the harsh consequences for his actions. The following 18 years of his life have been filled with preaching, fleeing, forsaking, imprisonment and torture. He suffered and cried much over the endangerment he brought to his family, yet as he says, "The love of Jesus forced me to go on."

One day in July 1981, Yun was in a village in the southern part of Henan province. He was meeting with several well-respected and faithful co-workers from the house church network in that area. Their conversation centered on the need to expose the TSPM church for what it was and to build the true Church of Christ by preaching the Gospel. They were planning new thrusts forward for the sake of evangelizing.

It was a dark windy night and the clouds hid the brightness of the stars. Yun preached with great eagerness about the cross of Christ, and His willingness to carry it. Like the first apostles, they must be willing to suffer and be martyrs for the sake of the Gospel. Over one hundred believers had gathered. They were deeply touched by the message.

Suddenly the sound of motor engines cut through the night air and into the meeting room. Gunshots from several weapons were heard. More than thirty policemen with batons, ropes and pistols, stormed into the courtyard. At once, they recognized Brother Yun, the troublemaker. They took hold of him, put him in iron chains, and forced him to kneel in the middle of the room. The couple who lived in the house where the meeting took place were also handcuffed. The Chinese police are well known for their brutality, and violence. They're not afraid of brutalizing their suspects by beatings or even shooting them to death!

Several Christians who protested were immediately kicked and beaten so hard they fell to the floor, and then were tied up. They continued to punch Yun and tried to force him to tell who was organizing the meeting. He told them he was the only one responsible, but another man came forward and took the responsibility for this meeting. The police were infuriated by this, and started to beat them unmercifully. Except for a few elderly women, all of them were exposed to hard beatings. After they had obtained all the names and addresses, the police released all the people, except for Yun and a few others. They were thrown into a police car to be taken to jail.

However, the policemen in their haste had forced too many people into the police car so that the tires began to go flat. Rather then be stranded out in the country in the middle of the night, the police ordered Yun and several others out of the car and instructed them to report to the police station at once. They believed he and the others would not have the courage to try to escape, so they kicked them out of the car and drove on.

This was the opportunity God had given him to escape! But at the same time he began to complain to the Lord as he walked alone in the darkness, "My God, my God, why have they treated me this way? Why did You not protect me?" God then reminded him of this scripture: "To this you were called, because Christ suffered for you, leaving you an example, that you should follow in His steps." (1 Peter 2:21)

And again, these words came to him: "You shall go to the west and to the south and preach the gospel. Turn around, for the Kingdom of God is near.... When you are persecuted in one place, escape to another."

Of course, he did not go to the police station. The slogan of the Christians in China's house churches is that they always have to be ready to escape, preach and suffer for the Gospel. Yun accepted that this was his lot in life.

He travelled to another area to minister, where he was soon recognized by the police as one who was "creating trouble and social disorder in the whole region." When the police found out that several of the arrested people did not appear at the station, they were furious and went over to their homes, including Yun's. Everything was thoroughly searched through, and their belongings confiscated. Yun's wife was so fearful that she dared not go home. The police had even taken Yun's mother to the police station for questioning.

When a Christian or pastor is arrested in China, his entire family suffers. The police will often take all the belongings of the family, even the food, and the family is left destitute. In school, the children are treated unfairly by the teachers and other pupils.

Yun became one of the most wanted criminals by the police. Posters with pictures of him decorated walls, telephone poles and other notice boards. Even though he was only in his early twenties, the police regarded him as the one in charge of the "illegal house churches in the province." He was accused of instigating social unrest, being a contra-revolutionary who was unwilling to obey the official church, and submit himself under the Three-Self system.

This was exactly right. Yun says, "Our preachers are totally different from those who are supported by the government and the Three-Self Church. It is not a strange thing that the security police are charging us with instigating social unrest, and for preaching another Jesus than the official church. Jesus said to us, "Be not afraid, little flock. Preach the Word of Life everywhere to your Chinese countryman, even when you suffer."

During his first ten years after becoming a Christian, Yun was arrested several times, but he always managed to escape before the police managed to interrogate him and find out anything. One Christmas Eve he and his wife, Deling, and a few others were on their way to an important meeting. At a bus station he was recognized by a policeman who grabbed Yun's jacket collar and commanded, "Follow me!" He also snatched Deling's handbag and her Bible. Suddenly, Yun heard very clearly the voice of the Holy Spirit commanding him to, "RUN!"

Yun responded with a loud cry, "Run!" At the same time he pulled away from the policeman's grasp. He already had a slight lead before the policeman realized what had happened. The officer shouted, "Help! Catch that spy!" The people who watched what happened were in awe by what was going on. Yun and Deling had managed to escape.

Unfortunately, the police confiscated Deling's handbag. Among her belongings they found addresses to the places they were planning to visit. The police took action very quickly and investigated all the homes. They could not find Yun anywhere, but as compensation they arrested several local Christian leaders instead.

Chapter Eight

New Escape—"Peter's God is Your God"

In 1983 the Chinese government launched a campaign against those forces in the country that they referred to as "spiritual pollution." The government in its pronouncement stated that this included all "dangerous sects." But what defined a so-called dangerous sect? Unfortunately, the government's perspective included all congregations outside of the Three-Self Patriotic Church as "dangerous spiritual pollutants." All over the country, Christians were arrested, and the leaders sentenced to severe punishment. The campaign also hit Yun and many of his friends and fellow-workers in Henan province.

At times, Yun would experience a strong sense of foreboding that something wrong was going to happen. One day, he prayed with several friends for confirmation of God's leading for his life and ministry. These friends shared that they had received a letter from the Christians in Shaanxi province, located west of Henan province. They were asking for someone to come and help them plant new churches and train their evangelists. One of Yun's friends' told him that since he had a calling to go to the west to preach and witness that this mission to Shaanxi belonged to nobody but Yun. Yun immediately responded that he was willing to go.

The night before he was to leave, he prayed for a long time with his friends. Suddenly, a terrible vision of darkness appeared to him. A creature with a horrible face came against him. At the same time Yun shouted, "Hallelujah! We overpower you by Jesus' blood. Jesus has won!" After the vision had ended, the others asked him what had happened. Yun told them that a monster forced him to the ground, and sat on him. "It tried to seal my mouth closed with its hands. Then, when I had nearly lost my breath, I saw an angel flying towards me. With all of my strength, I poked my fingers into the eyes of the monster. It fell to the ground, and I flew away with the angel."

The next day, Yun set out again—by bus for his destination of Shaanxi. The local leaders from several counties were to join together for a three-day meeting in the mountain area of the province. By the second day of meetings Yun lost his voice, and had to rest. He was led to a house located close to where the meetings were taking place. He laid down to get some rest.

BANG! The door to the room was knocked down, and three policemen came running in and tied Yun up with ropes. Just as they were about to leave the room they discovered a red wooden cross on the wall. On it was written, "God loves all people." The policemen laughed loudly—

they had an idea! Perhaps they should tie this cross to Yun's back. The landlord came and told them Yun had done nothing wrong, and that they could take him instead. The policemen answered him by kicking and beating him up.

This took place in a rather deserted mountain area. The people, who lived there, had little contact with the outside world. They had never seen travellers before who were evangelists. So the police procession with this stranger, arrested, and tied up with a large red cross on his back, was a remarkable sight, and many followed along. In front of them, a slow moving car drove along, and using loudspeakers, kept repeating, "This man came from Henan to speak about Jesus. He has destabilized the social order, and many have been frightened. Now he has been arrested, and we are going to punish him severely!"

And this is exactly what they did—by pure physical force they hit him with clenched fists from all sides as well as kicking him. Yun nearly fainted. Soon his face was covered with blood. When he looked up, he saw people who stood by the road. They cried and pitied him, because they thought he was being treated so badly. Yun asked them not to cry for him, but for the souls of their people.

At the police station, he was thrown into a large interrogation room, with iron bars on the windows and door. The Holy Spirit gently reminded him, "Your Father will protect you." Two officers started the interrogation. Yun told them he was from Henan province. After answering their basic questions, he only mumbled in response and glared intensely at them. The officers believed he was a crazy man. Outside, in the courtyard, a group of curious onlookers were gathered, and they peeped in through the window as if they were spectators at a play.

One of the officers left the interrogation room to call the police in Henan province for information on Yun. Then the other policeman left. Yun was now alone. The Holy Spirit spoke to Yun saying, "Peter's God is your God." Instantly, he remembered how the angels had opened the gates of the prison for Peter. Several of the ropes tied around Yun suddenly snapped miraculously, although his hands were still bound together. Standing, he went to the door, which was unlocked, and with his mouth, grabbed the handle and pulled open the door.

He then walked through the crowd of people in the courtyard to the north end of the police station, and reminded himself that the blood of Christ protected him. No one in the crowd saw him. It was as if he was invisible. There he found a washroom, and managed to free his hands from the ropes. His hands having been tied so long were still numb. How could he climb over the wall to escape? As the Holy Spirit came upon him he exercised his authority in Jesus Christ and commanded his hands and arms to be restored. A miracle took place at that moment in his heart and body. He now realized that Peter's God was his God!

Then with a supernatural power, as if an angel lifted him up, he jumped up onto a high wall, which was covered with glass shreds and then down the other side. By this time darkness enveloped the path where he walked. He went a long way, stumbling and falling in the dark. He managed to cross over several hills and a river. After several hours, he suddenly heard somebody shout his name. The man shouting turned out to be a Christian from this area. He had been participating in the meetings, but left before Yun was caught by the police. Now, he was busy fertilizing his fields. He took Yun to a place where some people had gathered.

After a couple of hours of walking in the dark, they heard people crying and praying in the woods, praying for Yun.

Apparently they had been praying for Yun's release since he had been arrested. Now as he stood there, in the midst of them, they could hardly believe their eyes. What Yun had seen in the vision before he traveled west, had happened. The monster had lost. God had set him free from evil men, in a miraculous way. The brothers helped wash his wounds, and then he left—to continue to preach, teach and experience more escapes.

Chapter Nine

"Look Toward Jerusalem"

"During those days when I was preaching and escaping, God gave me so much comfort and support! Therefore I was also able to comfort and inspire my co-workers," states Yun. Together they would comfort, encourage and pray for each other. This is the way the body of Christ functioned. It was an army on its way to destroy the works of Satan, and proclaim the Kingdom of God. Yet for the evangelists, this meant separation from their families, persecution, humiliation, and beatings. But nevertheless, they rejoiced in the Lord who was with them—and they also experienced true fellowship with their brethren in the ministry.

There were many prophecies that new territories would be won for the Gospel. In 1982 and 1983 the fire of the Gospel burned with power in the provinces of Shaanxi and Hubei. At the same time, new waves of persecution were approaching.

The evangelists in China often use bicycles to go from place to place. In 1982, Yun was cycling southwards to the province of Hubei, with several co-workers. One of them, sister Ding, had received several songs from the Holy Spirit. One song went like this:

"Looking ahead to the West,
The expansive fields are deserted.
The heart of the Lord grieves daily,
Who will go ahead for the Lord?
Our eyes full of tears,
Blood boiling in our veins,
Carrying the heavy cross,
Go! Save the Lost Sheep."

Again it was going westward that mattered. The song expressed a clear direction regarding God's will. They should look to the west, in the direction of Jerusalem. This young sister sang what God was calling them to do. Yun felt God prompting him to tell his fellow workers this: "With the little strength we have, we need to follow the example of the congregation in Philadelphia, which did not spare themselves in spreading the salvation of the Gospel."

As the number of believers increased, Satan continued with his schemes. In the border district between Henan and Hubei, many evangelists were arrested. Undercover police monitored the border patrol, bus and railway stations. However, Yun and his fellow workers continued to spread the Gospel, and they sang this song:

"Go forward! Follow the Lord; never look back.
Go forward! Follow Jesus; advancing, never retreat.
No one who puts his hands to the plow and looks back,
Is fit for the kingdom of God!"

The security police increased their attack on the house churches throughout the regions of Hubei province. Posters were placed everywhere declaring that the house churches must be crushed. Radio stations broadcast to the populace the message that all evangelists from Henan were to be arrested.

The weather that they faced underlined the persecutions that waited. An icy, cold wind from Siberia settled upon northern China. Many of those who usually accommodated the travelling evangelists were also arrested. Up until now the evangelists were warmly welcomed in ordinary homes to share food and shelter. But many became afraid for the safety of their families. In some villages, the evangelists were denied access because of the brutality of the police towards those who had helped them.

A woman knelt down in front of them, and begged them to leave. "Our home can not receive you. Please, go to another place!" Yun asked, with tears in his eyes, if she could give them a quilt to cover themselves. They needed something to keep warm from the cold wintry wind. But the woman did not dare to give them anything for fear the police might trace the blanket back to her. The evangelists could not find any place to stay. For the next several nights they tried to take shelter from the wind as they lived out in the wilderness—frozen, hungry and lightly dressed.

In the cold darkness of the stormy night, they would sing hymns to keep their courage up. One of the women found shelter inside a haystack. Yun and another brother hid in the bush by a lake. It helped a little, yet they could not keep the cold out. As the temperature continued to fall, the winds increased. The stormy showers cut like icy nails, right to the bone, through their flimsy clothing. The two friends clung to each other, trying to keep warm. While they lay there, hungry and with chattering teeth, they prayed for their people.

"Oh Lord! We pray that You will drive back the dark clouds from China. For the sake of Your blood—have mercy on our country and with our people!"

As they sang Yun felt anger and bitterness growing in his heart. Finally he cried out, "My God! I have my mother and my wife at home. How could You treat me in this way?" But God kept silent, even though Yun poured out all his pent up anger.

He desired to go back home, yet he kept on going. Gradually, he realized that the Lord was using adversity and suffering to form him. It was then that he was able to overcome his bitter thoughts and feelings. A new song began to form in his mind and heart:

"As long as I live, I will love my Lord only.
With all my heart, all my strength, all my talents,
I will love my Lord only.
No matter what happens, I will love my Lord only.
In speech and in action, through all my life,
I will love my Lord only."

The images of Christ being crucified flooded his mind and he heard the voice of the Lord saying, "I have loved you with an eternal love, and I will never leave you."

Yun committed to memory all the songs and visions he received and everything he experienced. He continually reminded himself of all that God had said and done for him. For that reason, he is today able to remember it all so clearly, so many years later.

Yun often quotes this scripture, "Whoever serves me must follow me; and where I am, my servant also will be. My Father will honor the one who serves me." (John 12:26)

Chapter Ten

MORE TROUBLE IS WAITING

Yun sensed in his spirit that he would be facing a time of great suffering soon. This suffering would come in order to equip him for the great calling God had for him. One Christian brother prayed for him and prophesied, "My Son, regardless of the circumstances, always have your eyes on Jesus, praise Him, and give Him honor."

Yun called all the house church leaders from the south of Henan and the north of Hubei for a meeting. During their gathering Yun felt led to read from Acts 20:22-38. Here the apostle Paul announces that he must go to Jerusalem as the Holy Spirit has forewarned him that chains, tribulations and persecutions await him.

By the time he had finished reading these verses the workers were all crying loudly. There were many prophecies given during their time together which told Yun that there was much suffering ahead for him. The next day, Yun and his wife, Deling, traveled by bus in a northerly direction. At the bus station they saw placards calling for his arrest. It was a strange feeling for Yun to read this; after all he was a wanted man by the police. Below his picture was a description, which described him as a dangerous criminal. According to the police, Yun was labeled as a leader of a reactionary group involved in anti-revolutionary activities. He was classified a troublemaker, charged with provoking Christians to break the law.

Yun was wearing dark sunglasses as he and Deling overheard waiting passengers discussing the wanted posters for Yun. It would certainly mean a lot of money for the individual who could give the police the information they needed to arrest Yun.

On their journey they met a Christian woman who had been visiting her husband in the prison. He had been arrested for preaching the Gospel. Her husband had been treated very badly, and she hardly recognized him because of the inhuman treatment he had faced in prison. He was emaciated, and quite sick. Yun and Deling prayed and cried with this dear woman. Overcome by compassion, Deling gave her all the money they had.

When they arrived at their destination in northeast Henan, they soon discovered how tense the situation was. In his heart Yun continued to sing,

"And now, forced by the Spirit, I will go to Jerusalem!
I do not know what is waiting for me there.
But I count my life for nothing,
If I only can finish the race,
And do the task, which the Lord Jesus Christ has given me,

To be a witness about the grace of God."

Even in this region atheistic slogans were plastered everywhere. Placards calling for the arrest of Christians and the crushing of the house churches were evident for all to see. But the brothers and sisters in this area had no fear whatsoever. Facing the risk of imprisonment and adversity, they willingly gave shelter to the evangelists. The workers from several areas had gathered despite the risk of arrest. One of the workers, a prayer warrior, prophesied that, "during the next three days, some of us will be caught, and some will even be martyrs."

Nevertheless they kept their courage up by praying and singing. They were warriors who did not want to surrender the prize, but run to finish the race. Yun shared a message about martyrdom and suffering for the sake of the Gospel. Everyone sang, "I am willing to die for the Lord." Yun and his wife decided that she, Deling, should return home to visit and comfort the families of the many workers who had recently been imprisoned.

It was a snowy winter in 1983 as they met together for these three days. Yet the warmth of Jesus Christ glowed in their hearts. At midnight of the third day, the meeting concluded. The sisters had prepared a dish with hot water to wash one another's feet. With tears in his eyes, Yun started to wash the feet of his workers. After he finished, they asked him to sit on a chair. They took off his shoes and socks, and washed his feet, dried them, and put on his shoes. Then they went out into the snow and cold weather to retire for the evening to their billeted homes.

Before they parted, a man who Yun had spent much time together with took a scarf and put it around Yun's neck. It was to protect him against the cold.

These meetings took place in a village called "The Village of Love." What was about to happen in the next few days contradicted everything this name stood for.

Chapter Eleven

The Heavenly Man

As they walked out into the dark cold wintry night, several searchlights pointed at them. They immediately sensed danger. A man approached Yun and in a threatening manner shouted, "Who are you? What's your business here?"

Some of the Christians turned and fled. Yun also tried to escape, when a police officer took hold of him, and put an electric prod against his body. Powerful electric currents ran through him. The pain was terrible. He fell into the snow unable to move. Several policemen hit him with their rifle butts, and tied him up. Instantly, Yun heard a voice from above say two words to him, "I know!"

Lying in the snow, he recalled the words of the Lord to the church in Smyrna in the book of Revelation. "I know your afflictions and your poverty—yet you are rich! I know the slander of those who say they are Jews and are not, but are a synagogue of Satan. Do not be afraid of what you are about to suffer. I tell you, the devil will put some of you in prison to test you, and you will suffer persecution for ten days. Be faithful, even to the point of death, and I will give you the crown of life." (Revelation 2:9)

All his pain and fear vanished. A policeman started threatening him. If he refused to tell who they were and who he was meeting with, he would be killed. Yun was not afraid to lose his life, but he was concerned for his fellow workers and their security. Maybe some of the Christians had not been informed about the arrests. He had to warn them of the situation. He was determined not to give away any information about who he was or about anybody else. He remembered how David in the Bible acted as a madman when he met with Abimelech.

When the police questioned Yun, he answered with a statement that has now become his nickname. He shouted out "I am a heavenly man, and I live in the village of the Gospel. My name is Morning Star. My father's name is Full of Grace. My mother's name is Faith, Hope and Love."

Filled with hatred and anger, another policeman started kicking him. He pulled Yun up and hissed in his face, saying, "What is it you are muttering about? I asked you who you are, and where you come from, and where your fellow workers are?" Yun pointed to the east saying, "In that village over there." The policeman responded, "Walk in front of me. If you make trouble, I will skin you alive."

Yun repeated that he was only a heavenly man. Then he started to shout aloud to give a warning to the others in the area. He continued shouting; "I've been caught by the security police! I am a heavenly man, and I don't know where the meetings took place!"

They brought him to one of the villages, and a policeman took hold of him and snarled, "Which house?" Yun pretended to be surprised and shouted out loud, "Oh, it's not in this village! It must be the other village!" Yun pointed in an entirely different direction. At this point, the policemen were furious, they felt he had made a fool of them. They threw him to the ground, kicking and hitting him, again and again and again. Then they used their electric prods to shock his body so that pain ripped through him. If God had not protected him, they would have killed him right there.

His friends, standing a safe distance away, cried when they saw how badly Yun was being treated. Yun shouted out, "I am the heavenly man. I don't know where this meeting was. I only know heavenly men. I don't know who you are. The heavenly man will never become a Judas."

The police locked Yun up in a cell with four other Christian brothers. Outside it was 10 to 15 degrees below zero with a cold piercing wind blowing, making it ice cold inside the prison cell. The cell had no form of heating and what made matters worst, the police had taken Yun's overcoat and thrown it into the snow when he was first arrested. He shivered like a leaf, soon his hands and feet were numb from the cold.

Yun began hitting the iron bars with his handcuffs. Then he discovered a broken wooden trunk in the cell, which contained a drum. Raising his hands he began to strike the drum making a loud booming noise. He began to sing, Psalm 150, "Praise the Lord. Praise God in his sanctuary; praise Him in his mighty heavens.... Praise Him with the sounding of the trumpet, praise Him with the harp and lyre."

As he jumped around dancing and singing, the coldness left him! He continued singing other Psalms as well. The other brothers in the cell were on their knees praying. The guards certainly believed they had a crazy man in the prison, and left him alone. All night long, Yun was beating on this drum, praising the Lord with a loud voice. Yun and his brothers felt tremendously encouraged.

Chapter Twelve

Persecution and Torture

The next day the other prisoners were sent out to shovel snow. Not Yun, he was to be punished for his behaviour in the cell. "You caused a terrible uproar all night long. This will cool you down," said one of the police officers.

A policeman took an electric prod and waved it in front of Yun's face. Then he commanded him to kneel down, but Yun refused and said, "I will only kneel down before my Lord and my God." The officer snarled at him: "I am your God. If you kneel down now, I can set you free immediately."

Yet, Yun had new courage and he said, "In the name of Jesus, you are not my God! You are only a policeman. My God is in heaven. I am a heavenly man."

The policeman snarled and switched on the power button, "If you are a heavenly man, you do not need to be afraid of this, do you?" Several policemen came over to Yun, grabbed his arms and forced him to hold the staff with his hands. The electricity hit his body with devastating power. It felt like his heart would burst. He shouted, "Jesus! Have mercy on me!" At that same moment, the instrument of torture suddenly malfunctioned. It would no longer work! The policemen looked at the staff in bewilderment, and then quickly left the room.

Following this episode of torture, Yun and one other, Brother Jian, were put in a cell with ten criminals. Over the following days, Yun was repeatedly beaten, again and again by these ten criminals. The prison guards encouraged the prisoners to harass Yun in any way, even by stepping on his chest. Many times he was beaten so badly that blood came through his nose and mouth. Still, he refused to say anything.

Gradually over time the attitude among his fellow prisoners changed. One of them told the others that Yun was not crazy, but a good man willing to pay a high price for his convictions. He helped Yun in the cell, and after his release, he became an ardent Christian.

The police soon realized they had caught a "big fish" in Yun, but who was he? Despite being brutally beaten, Yun never told them who he was or the names and addresses of his workers. In desperation, the PSB began to contact the police in Yun's home province seeking information that would help them identify who he was.

Finally after several weeks, police from Yun's home county arrived at the prison. They immediately recognized him. This was now their opportunity to seek revenge, after all, Yun had played them for a fool one too many times. Their cruel nature would soon be unleashed.

Yun was led to a prison van. As usual, they kicked him with their boots and hit him with their batons and fists. He had several wounds, and his body ached. Upon getting into the back of the vehicle they hung him by his handcuffs, leaving him to dangle. The handcuffs cut into his wrists, right to the bone. This was the beginning of a long and painful drive for Yun. Each time the van turned, his body would swing and hit the side of the van. The handcuffs steadily cut even deeper and deeper. The pain was excruciating, but there was nothing he could do to ease it.

During their trip, the police poked his body with their electric prod shocking him with the electric current. Swaying back and forth, he was like a helpless animal waiting to be slaughtered. His entire body was covered with blood. He began to doubt God's promise to protect him. He shouted to God and begged to die, "Oh, Lord Jesus! Why do you let me go through this pain? Please, forgive me! Receive my soul."

Unexpectedly, the doubt, fear and pain were replaced by the comforting presence of God as his mind was directed to Psalm 46, "Be still, and know that I am God; I will be exalted among the nations, I will be exalted in the earth."

When the van arrived in one of the towns in his home county, he discovered slogans plastered all over by the PSB stating, "Congratulations on the arrest of the contra revolutionary Yun. Down with the reactionary Yun and his fellow workers! Act very hard against these illegal Christian meetings, which are led by Yun".

Chapter Thirteen

THE FAST BEGINS

The PSB van stopped by the gate of the prison. A policeman kicked Yun out of the van who was already in a terrible condition. This thin, barefooted, manhandled, little man was led into the interrogation room, where a dozen policemen stood waiting for him.

"So you are the one calling yourself 'the heavenly man'? Not bad, not bad at all. Now your destiny is in our hands. You will not be a free man until you've got your punishment. By now you must have realized that you were wrong. All your co-workers are also in our hands." He named off several names and continued, "You have been defeated. This illegal religion of yours is crushed, finished. You will not avoid being punished, you are the eternal enemy of the party and the people!"

Yun felt indignation rising within him, but he kept

silent. The Spirit of the Lord comforted him with these words, "Through suffering the Gospel is reaching out to every person on earth. The truth has reached millions of hearts. Truth will always remain truth."

An interrogator with a menacing look came towards Yun, "Have you had enough, or is more treatment necessary? Your crimes are so many and they are very serious. But the party is always ready to be kind to somebody who admits their wrongdoings, and harsh towards those who deny doing wrong." He continued promising Yun complete freedom, if only he would expose the house church, its structure and activities. "If you co-operate with us, I can guarantee that you will be home with your family before the spring festival starts," he said.

As Yun listened to his interrogator, he knew what he wanted to say to him, "You are promising me release and freedom, but I can assure you, you are all going to die. Where are you going after death? You must accept Christ as your Savior."

Yun responded by asking if he could have time to think it over. He told his interrogator that he had suffered much during the past few days through beatings, torture and hunger and that he could hardly speak. He needed time to think, rest and recuperate. The interrogator, taken in by Yun's logic agreed.

Sitting in his prison cell he sensed that God had allowed him to go to prison to deepen his relationship with Him. He remembered how Jesus had fasted to overcome the temptations he was exposed to. The more that Yun thought of this, he knew he had to make a drastic decision. He later shared that, "The Holy Spirit and I made a collective decision. That decision was to follow Jesus' example in the same way that he had fasted in the desert to overcome the temptations."

So began Yun's period of fasting and prayer. He focused his time of prayer on the various needs confronting him; from the urgency to spread the Gospel, to praying for the suffering Church and the millions of lost souls who needed salvation, to the precious brothers and sisters who like him were now in prison.

This was a very difficult thing for him to do for several reasons. First, hunger gnawed at him from the days of already going without food. Secondly, to make it even worse, the Chinese spring festival had begun.

During this time, the prison governor showed a measure of compassion towards the prisoners, by allowing them more food to eat. The smell of pork and celery floated through the corridors, and into the cells—an almost irresistible temptation!

His stomach rumbled with hunger, and he was tempted to eat. A thought came to him, "This festival is only once a year. You should eat only a little bit." Besides, he had been tortured and harassed and had not eaten for several days. It couldn't harm anyone if he only took a small bit of food.

In contrast to this, an even stronger thought occurred to him, "You have to be firm, and resist the devil and he will then flee from you!" He thought of Jesus' long fast in the desert and shouted out, "In the name of the Lord Jesus Christ, hunger pains leave me!"

He then gave his bread and soup to the man who the prison guards had appointed to be the leader in their cell. He told him he was not hungry and encouraged him to divide his food with the others. Once he gave his food away, his strong feelings of hunger disappeared.

For a prisoner in China, the stomach is his god, and the food his lord. This is how the other prisoners began to appreciate Yun. They wanted to know why a good and warm-hearted man like him could end up in prison. He answered, by telling them that God had chosen him to preach the Gospel of Jesus Christ.

After that, they asked him to sing about Jesus. He did, and then he was able to preach to them about Jesus and their need for salvation. They appreciated what they heard, even if they did not understand much of what he said. He told them to divide his food between them since he could not eat, and he asked them not to tell the prison guards about this. This was of course, very much appreciated by the prisoners.

His days in prison slipped by while he memorized portions of the scripture. He thought about the many Christians who had suffered for the sake of the Gospel. The words of God filled his mind, and he did not touch any food. Fear and bitterness left, and joy and peace surrounded him. Never again would he hate those who had tortured and abused him. What they did to him, in a way, was the will of God. The Lord had allowed him to be tested.

Yun wanted to be like Jesus—not to fight back when he was beaten and scorned. Revenge belongs to God. He used the Word of God repeatedly to fight the attacks of the enemy. The greatest weapon he had were the words the Lord gave him, "Be silent. Put your trust in the Lord. Don't be afraid. Just believe. Don't look at the circumstances. Don't look at yourself. Trust in the Lord. Pray more, and you will see the Glory of God."

It was a promise of freedom for his future.

Chapter Fourteen

The Gates of Iron Shall be Opened

After Yun had fasted forty days and forty nights in prison, Satan tempted him by asking, "Are you trying to outdo your Master? He only fasted for forty days and forty nights. Why doesn't God help you? You will certainly die. And then what will happen to your family, your mother and your wife?"

The constant attack upon his mind intensified as a spiritual darkness seemed to surround him. Questions and fears plagued his thinking. Was his pride motivating him to fast?

Yun didn't know how to handle the pressure, and considered taking his own life. But he knew that doing so would be a terrible sin, so he kept on fighting and resisting these tormenting thoughts until he was able to find his comfort in God's Word.

He shouted out in faith, "Do not exult over me, you

foe! Even if I sit in the dark, the Lord is my light. He will lead me out into the light. I will see His justice."

His struggles continued. Joy and peace alternated with despair, pain and fear. The outward circumstances that he faced were beyond his ability to cope. Now he began to question whether the inner peace of God that had held him securely for years was now leaving him. After a long night of struggle, he asked God, "Lord, have I sinned? What have I done to you? Why don't you forgive my sins?" In desperation, he shouted to Jesus, "Receive my spirit!"

Yet again, God spoke to him, "My son! I know your deeds. I know how little strength you have. You have kept my Word, and not forsaken my Name." Upon hearing this Yun started crying with joy. He felt like a child who had been badly manhandled, and now God's care and true love surrounded him. He then heard these words which would soon turn out to be prophetic: "See, I have placed before you an open door, that no one can shut. I know that you have little strength, yet you have kept my word, and have not denied my name." (Rev. 3:8)

These words were followed by a powerful vision from God. The heavenly man saw several iron doors that opened up to him, one after another. Through them he saw countless men and women, of different nationalities, both young and old, worshipping the Lord. The Holy Spirit then reminded him of the visions that he had received earlier in his life concerning his calling to be an evangelist.

After this, once again, depressing clouds of torment descended upon him. He saw no possibilities of preaching the Gospel and fulfilling his calling. In his despair he expressed to God that, "Even if You opened up the gates of the prison, I would have no strength to walk out."

The Lord reminded him that "My calling is irreversible. Everyone who believes, can do what I have done. Yes, they shall do even greater things than this." All the pain and hurt disappeared. Light, strength and joy flooded his heart. He received another vision where God allowed him to see himself and other believers breaking through every barrier and difficulty that they faced.

Those in the prison started to talk about this man, who went without food and still lived. The prisoners started to make bets on how long he would live. A fellow prisoner, whose task it was to carry him to and from the interrogation room, felt pity for him once he saw the wounds and Yun's emaciated body.

As he suffered in prison, the other prisoners' interest in him increased, causing them to ask, "What does this man's life stand for?" Outside the prison, the believers were aware of Yun's suffering and fearless uncompromising trust in God. Many Christians in the house churches fasted and prayed day and night for him. And all the while the churches kept on growing. Signs and wonders continued, and thousands of new Christians were added to the Body of Christ.

Chapter Fifteen

THE TEMPTATION

As Yun continued to fast and pray he experienced a horrible vision. In it, he saw a powerful desert storm rip the roof off his house. The foundation of his home stood firm, but the walls became crooked and cracked. From the cracks in the walls, large numbers of scorpions, black snakes, and swarms of wasps attacked him. Fear took hold of Yun. He didn't know what to do.

In the vision he turned around and saw a naked woman, who opened up her bosom. She invited him to seek refuge in her, "Come here, escape together with me." The storm and all the terrible reptiles prompted him to run towards the naked woman, this prostitute, in order to avoid the coming catastrophe. Suddenly, he saw his mother standing there, her face shining, and he stopped. She gave him a piece of bread, and asked him to eat it. The wasps, scorpions, and black snakes then started to attack him again. Their bites felt like thousands of arrows penetrating his heart. He twisted in pain and cried out, "Oh God! Save me!" and woke up.

Yun now understood that new interrogations were to follow, and he stretched his hand out to Brother Li, who was beside him. "I am going to be interrogated again, and I am going to suffer for the name of the Lord. Please, pray for mercy and help!" Just then the hinges screeched when the steel door to his cell opened. A loud voice broke the silence, "Bring Yun out!"

Brother Li used to help Yun in many ways. At times he carried him to and from his interrogations when Yun couldn't walk. Before prison, Li was a ruthless robber. The police had placed him in Yun's cell, telling him to keep Yun under surveillance and report everything he did to the prison guards. But Li became curious about this man, Yun, and why he suffered so badly when his behavior was so upright. One day Li asked to know Jesus as his Savior. Now at last, Yun had a Christian Brother as a roommate.

Yun was placed on the cement floor in the interrogation room. One of his interrogators asked if he was going to remain silent today. "We've got methods that have made even tougher men than you talk," he sneered. And then the brutality began. They stepped on his hands and his feet, and the two men in charge of his interrogation brought out their electric prods. They shocked Yun's head, face, and several other parts of his body with electric currents, using the maximum setting on their torturous tool. The electrical shock to his body was excruciating. With the Word of God lodged in his heart, he knew that the Lord stood by his side. The pain softened, to a degree. They did not get one single word out of him.

Due to Yun's resistance they changed their tactics and put on their 'silk-glove' approach. The interrogation leader told Yun, "We have given you a chance. If you admit that you have done wrong, and worked-up the Christians to go against the party and the registered Church, we will ignore what you've done. We will even consider making you a member of the party! You may even become a chairman for the Three-Self Church!" He gave Yun a friendly kick. "Now, what do you say?"

Yun's horrible vision came flooding back to him. Now he understood who the naked prostitute woman was, who it was that was enticing and offering him protection from the terrible reptiles. Supposedly, he could avoid the humiliation, the pain, and be set free. How wonderful it would be to go home to his wife. All he needed to do was to surrender his calling, come under the authority of the Three-Self Church and follow their instructions.

The torture, the hunger, the dirt, the smell, and everything else of this evil prison would come to an end, and hopefully fade from his memory. They promised that he could preach, baptize people, and teach them from the Bible. He could even have a church building with songbooks, and more Bibles than he could imagine. Nothing would be held back from him. At last his family would be safe and he would have a good secure position.

Quickly his mind raced to the question, "What were the conditions he would have to agree to?" How difficult would it be to say 'yes' to the church that he considered a prostitute? 'Yes,' to being controlled and directed by the communist party?

Startled, he heard the interrogator ask, "Do you hear me, Yun? Do you accept this offer?" At once, Yun recognized the words of his tormentors. To agree with them would compromise his calling and his life. No longer would he be a free bird, he would then be one held inside a cage.

An agonizing war escalated within the heart of this 25-year-old young man. He could not let them beat him to death. There was so much to live for. He was young, married, had many friends and responsibilities. His entire life was ahead of him.

Just as he was about to give in, and say 'yes,' the image of the naked prostitute appeared in his mind again. She waved her hand towards him, and the scorpions, snakes and swarms of wasps emerged again. He lay on the cold cement floor, half-dead, without the strength to speak.

Then the chief interrogator sent for someone from the medical clinic. An evil and merciless man, who was probably a doctor, came in and Yun heard him say, "Please leave the room. I will examine Yun alone." It turned out to be an examination that was out of the ordinary.

The doctor cruelly said, "I am sure this will make you talk." He put Yun on a table, and strapped his arms and his legs. With a malicious smile on his face, the doctor brought out several large needles. Apparently, he only used them for giving 'special' treatments to those who were unwilling to talk. Yun groaned and shrieked in pain as the 'doctor' pushed the thick needles under his fingernails, one after another. Yun passed out from the pain.

Later, Yun woke up in his cell. His entire body was numb, and he had no sense of feeling in his hands. Brother Li had heard the doctor say to him, "Yun, you pigheaded idiot! Go to your God!" The doctor told the others in the cell what kind of treatment Yun had been exposed to. Everyone was horrified. Even the toughest men in the cell—who used to torment Yun—were touched by Yun's ordeal.

The routine interrogations continued, with more beatings, electric shock torments and needles. In the midst of his horrendous torture, Yun believed God had something to tell him. Yun realized that he was strong willed. Through these evil man he learned incredible obedience, trust and hope in God. At the same time, his endurance was built up. His insight into the suffering of Christ and the greatness of the Kingdom of God increased.

Like Jesus in front of Pilate, he kept silent when he was interrogated, and didn't give away any information. As a teenager growing up, God had given him a song—to never become a Judas. He never did.

Chapter Sixteen

Suffering in Silence Where Wickedness Abounds

Their tactics of interrogation changed when they realized that Yun would give them no information. With great contempt they began to abuse his body by pulling his eyelids, his lips, his ears and other body parts. They would take off his clothes, and severely beat him. Then they would ask Brother Li to take him back to his cell.

Even the other prisoners thought this was too much. The interrogators again changed their tactics to stop the other prisoners from taking Yun's side. They started slandering and lying about Yun to the prisoners, saying that he was a political reactionary criminal who had misused the party's confidence.

They accused him of trying to fool them through trickery by not eating and pretending to be sick. When they had taken him to a hospital to get medical treatment the doctors openly stated that there was nothing wrong with him. Prison officials openly declared that Yun was an enemy of the state needing to be severely punished. It was now the duty of every prisoner in Yun's cell to keep him under strict observation and report his activity to the prison guards.

Cleverly they used Mao's theory of the class struggle to create hatred and mistrust against Yun. Up to this point, the prisoners serving long prison sentences were sympathetic to Yun. After hearing these accusations against Yun they became enraged against this defenseless poor creature. They had nothing to lose. They had been humiliated and treated unfairly so many times that they were regarded not as human beings. By harassing Yun, they were given the opportunity of venting their frustrations. The humiliation and the pain, which they brought upon Yun, had no limits.

In the beginning they were content with just insulting him. They despised the Jesus that he served. When this did not work they moved his 'bed' down beside the urinal in the cell. As there were 16 prisoners using the urinal, it is hard to imagine the terrible stench that filled the air as Yun lay on his bed beside it. But that was not enough.

Now the prisoners wanted some entertainment, and the prison cell leader took command. He walked over to Yun and urinated over his head and face. Yun, unable to protect himself, just laid there, powerless, helpless, close to death—a man who was now only skin and bones. He could only suffer in silence, and think about the words that described Jesus. "When they hurled their insults at him, he did not retaliate; when he suffered, he made no threats. Instead, he entrusted himself to him who judges justly."(1 Peter 2:23)

Where wickedness abounds, only the imagination can set the limit for the most gruesome and evil of activities.

When the guards talked about serious treatment, they meant serious. They allowed the other prisoners to throw Yun into the toilet, which was in fact a kind of open-style latrine.

One guard with an electric prod, poked Yun while he soaked in the toilet water. Waves of pain racked his emaciated body, which now weighted only 30 kg. Reeling from the pain, Yun was forced to crawl on his hands and knees over the heap of human excrement. At the same time they kicked him repeatedly and put an electric prod into his mouth. When they turned the voltage on, the pain was unimaginable. At that point Brother Li felt it was going too far. He tried to pull Yun out from the toilet, but the others stopped him.

Yun heard Psalm 22 in his heart, "My strength is dried up like a potsherd, and my tongue sticks to the roof of my mouth; you lay me in the dust of death. Dogs have surrounded me; a band of evil man has encircled me, they have pierced my hands and my feet." (Psalm 22:15-16)

He lay there lifeless, but his spirit was not dead! Once again he heard God saying: "Rejoice and be glad, because great is your reward in heaven, for in the same way they persecuted the prophets who were before you." (Matthew 5:12)

It was now the beginning of March 1984, and the weather outside was warming. Lying beside the outhouse wall, still recovering from his ordeal, silence rained down upon Yun. The prison guards had left him alone for a while. Yet, he was not totally alone, Jesus and his angels surrounded him.

Yun's thoughts went back to the night before he was arrested, so many days ago. He remembered the many brothers and sisters as they had met together and washed each other's feet that night. He recalled his dear friend who had given him a scarf, saying, "This will keep you warm from the cold," just before the police had arrived. So many good people.

He started to sing Psalm 23; "The Lord is my shepherd... even if... even if... I walk through the valley of the shadow of death, I will fear no evil." Not until the evening did they allow his friend to carry him back to his prison cell.

Unknown to Yun, the senior prison guard had not yet finished his task of tormenting him. The cruelty in him created new ideas. Yun had bound his scarf around his waist, and at the end of it he had attached his mug. His family had given him the mug as a reminder of them. It was so precious to him.

The prison guard ordered the prisoners to throw the mug into the urinal. So they tore off his scarf and mug, and threw it into the toilet. Yun attempted to grab his mug and scarf, but the heartless guard took the mug from him again. He threw it back into the toilet, and urinated on it.

Yun stretched out his hand, took hold of the mug, and held it closely to his chest. It was all soiled with urine. His heart was filled by rage, and he wanted to curse these evil men, but no words came from his lips. Instead he heard other words inside of him, "Bless and do not curse, take no revenge... be not defeated by evil, but overcome evil with good."

While he was crying in anger, he blessed these men. He had no idea that they would soon suffer for their heartlessness. Brother Li, his Christian cellmate, was moved to another cell because he tried to protect Yun. The prisoners then resumed their tormenting of Yun by kicking, beating and urinating on his head and face.

The morning after Brother Li had been removed, some of the prisoners started to itch terribly. There were red spots and wounds all over their bodies. They had contracted scabies! The itching was so bad, that they could not sit still. Yet, Yun appeared unaffected.

His cellmates wanted to examine Yun to see if he had scabies as well. Ripping his shirt off they discovered no red spots—nothing! Amazingly, the first man to contract scabies in the prison cell was the cell leader. Those who were not yet infected believed that the best thing they could do was to stay away from him.

Instead, they moved Yun from being beside the toilet to right along side the cell leader, hoping Yun would catch it as well. Soon it spread to the others totally bypassing Yun who remained disease free. The parasites seemed to 'jump above' him, attacking the others.

Only one other prisoner besides Yun remained disease free. Because of this he became quite friendly towards Yun. One night, when he placed his blanket over Yun, Yun whispered to him that he had to accept Jesus as his Savior. At that moment the man received Jesus in his heart, and served Yun faithfully.

All this made a strong impression on his fellow prisoners, but they still didn't stop harassing Yun. The boss of the cell grabbed Yun's blanket, and gave him his. It was all covered with blood and parasites. In spite of this, Yun did not get ill.

Chapter Seventeen

A Visit and the End of the Fast

It was the spring of 1984. For many weeks now, Satan had tormented Yun, trying to break him. His body was close to being totally destroyed. Only through the strength of the Lord was Yun able to endure this horrendous experience.

Outside the prison walls, the house churches were exposed to large waves of persecution. All throughout the south of Henan, many top leaders were arrested. Yun's mother took the initiative to gather the congregations together to fast and pray for the prisoners. Every morning and night they cried out to God.

They tried to discover from the authorities what punishment awaited Yun. Some police said he would be sentenced to life imprisonment, while others believed he would receive the death penalty. When the relatives of Yun's wife heard this, they encouraged her to divorce Yun and find another man. They told her Yun would never come back alive.

Only Yun and Deling's mothers encouraged her to be strong in the Lord and wait for him, even though it was hard for her. Yun's mother and Yun's wife were like Ruth and Naomi. They prayed against and broke down many barriers.

Deling had a dream that she and Yun's mother were visiting him in the prison. Even though he looked like a scarecrow, he was in good spirits, full of joy and peace. In the dream he gave her a key and said, "This key can unlock every door!"

When she woke up she felt a tremendous urge to pray. Indeed prayer is the key that opens all closed doors. After describing her dream, she discovered his mother had also dreamt a similar dream. By now Yun had been fasting for 74 days! It was truly a miracle that he survived. This unusual time was filled with great struggle and difficulty. Yun experienced much fear and darkness in his life, but accompanying the evil were signs, visions, dreams, and revelations from the Lord. Through God's faithfulness, Yun had remained faithful and did not become a Judas.

Many times he told the Lord, "As long as the churches on the outside are not being hurt I am willing to carry the burden, endure the suffering, even to the death, for the sake of you, oh Lord."

During his fast, he had not received any information about his family or the house churches. The temptation to believe what the other prisoners were telling him, that he was going to die in the prison, became his battleground. In spite of these prisoners being infected with scabies, they continued to harass him. From a human perspective Yun's situation looked hopeless.

On March 6, 1984, Deling, and his mother were asked by the authorities to visit Yun in prison. The prison officials were hoping that Yun's family would convince him to start eating again. When Yun's family received this invitation, they immediately felt that it was going to be an extraordinary meeting.

On the morning of the appointed visit, the authorities attempted one more time to make him talk. They took him to the interrogation room and said to him, "Yun, this is your final chance. If you cooperate with us, everything will be okay." When they realized he was refusing to talk, they attacked him with the electric prod once again. Before long Yun was unconsciousness.

As he lay on the cold floor barely alive, he could feel warmth on his face and someone caressing him. He opened his eyes slowly, to see his mother embracing him. Her warm teardrops awakened him from unconsciousness. Surrounding him were eight members of his family and church, praying for his healing. At first Deling became frightened, not believing this could be her husband. He was completely unrecognizable, emaciated, and black and blue from repeated beatings. His clothes, smeared with blood, could hardly be called rags. But his mother recognized her son.

As his mother continued to pray for him, Yun began to feel the strength of the Lord surging through his body. Yun heard these words going through his mind, "Speak! It is my time." As he opened his mouth to speak, his sister covered his mouth with her hand. She was afraid Yun would say something to cause him to face extreme punishment later. The authorities were closely monitoring their meeting.

As he pushed her hand away, an authoritative voice burst from within him, "Not by kings, nor by men who cannot help you; it is better to take refuge in the Lord than to trust in princes. Firmly rely on the Lord; don't be afraid. Jesus is the way, the truth and the life."

As he grabbed the hand of his friend, Yun continued, "Brother, riches and honor cannot corrupt, nor poverty and obscurity divert, nor threats and violence bend, those who rely on the Lord Jesus Christ. Trust in Him in order to be a true man. Abba Father told me that you would come to see me today."

The prison guards were watching everything going on, but it was as though their ears were dull and their eyes clouded. Yun continued crying aloud, "Mother, your son is hungry! Your son is thirsty, but not for earthly bread and water, but for the souls of men. Mom, if you will go out and spread the gospel, saving souls, that will be my bread!"

After shedding many tears, Yun ate for the first time in 74 days. They shared together the Lord's Supper—biscuits and wine. Yun's family knew the importance he always placed on remembering Jesus' Last Supper. During this meal he said, "Mother, this may be the last meal we have together. Maybe I will be killed. If I have to die let it be so. I will always be faithful to the Lord. If it is God's will, Mother, Deling, brothers and sisters, then we will meet again in His kingdom."

His wife and mother passionately embraced him. Everyone cried. It was then that Deling announced she was five months pregnant.

As if awakening from a dream, the prison guards began to shout and bang the table. The visitors were told to leave immediately. Before they left, his mother spoke to Yun with great authority, "God wants you to be obedient to your mother. You will live and not die. You must eat! We all need you, your wife, me, and the whole family of God."

Still clinging to her son, the hardened security guards threw her to the floor and grabbed Yun. The iron doors locked with a bang, but Yun could still hear his mother yelling outside, "My son! Be strong and survive, live for the Lord!" Yun shouted back, "Mother! You must preach the Gospel, and ask the Church to pray and fast!" This angered the prison guard and he hit Yun in the face with his clenched fist.

Once again, upon returning to his cell, the prison guard started harassing Yun with more beatings. He threatened to kill him. The cell leader and the other prisoners talked derogatory about Yun's faith. A Muslim snarled at him, "You Christians believe in Jesus and are preaching His teachings. You set yourself up against the party, and not just that, the heavenly law judges such pigs like you."

Suddenly, these fellow prisoners were shocked when Yun stood up and announced to them, "Dear fellow prisoners! The Lord wants me to speak today, and you all have to listen carefully!" The prisoners were flabbergasted. What kind of power enabled this bag of bones of a scarecrow to stand and speak with such authority and strength?

"The Lord has sent me to this prison, and to this cell, for your sake. From the first day I placed my feet here, I've told you that I believe in Jesus, and that I am preaching in His Name. I have told you that He is the living God. Now, you've seen for over 70 days that I've not eaten or drank anything. Don't you understand that I am still alive because God has protected me?"

Yun continued, "God wanted to demonstrate that He is a living God, and that Jesus is alive! How long will you continue to do evil things? When the judgement comes, how will you escape the frightfulness of hell? But Jesus is willing to forgive you, if you all repent and turn to the Lord! Now, kneel down and ask Jesus to forgive your sins. If you don't do this, none of you will be able to escape from a merciless judgement and the eternal fire of hell!"

The cell leader was the first to respond. He threw himself down on his knees and shouted, "Yun! What shall I do?" A dozen prisoners, including the Muslim, knelt around him. They cried to the Lord for forgiveness.

Instantly these cruel prisoners—who had hardened their conscience, felt guilty towards Yun for the things they had done to him. But Yun forgave them, in the same way that Joseph had forgiven his brothers. He encouraged them by saying, "You had in mind to hurt me, but God wanted the best—to save the lives of many people!" He baptized them by sprinkling a bit of water on them and he discipled them. The entire atmosphere of the cell changed. The language and behavior of the prisoners was totally changed.

Outside the prison walls the churches stood firm in prayer, night and day. Many Christians became more courageous. The fear that had gripped their hearts disappeared. Great miracles started happening, and many people turned to the Lord. People with all kinds of sicknesses came to their meetings. There were people with serious psychological illnesses and those possessed with demons. Everyone was healed and set free. Even members of the communist party received Jesus as their Savior, and became witnesses for Christ.

Inside prison Yun continued to take care of the new believers and teach them about the Gospel. Previously, hatred and selfishness reigned. Now many prisoners all over the prison received Christ as their Savior.

Many miracles took place among the prisoners. One such story is told about a certain man sentenced to death. He was a murderer. No one cared for him and everyone avoided his presence. He was chained to the wall, and raved like a wild animal. He bit anyone who came close to him. He tried many times to commit suicide.

Yun felt compassion for this man, and started to take care of him. He washed his wounds, and gave this man his food to eat. Through these unexpected acts of kindness, the man became curious. This was the start of a friendship, and after a couple of weeks he received Jesus in his heart. The last part of his life here on earth was filled with peace and joy! His face glowed as he prayed and sang spiritual songs. He was so filled with gratefulness. Like the forgiven robber on the cross, he entered death fearlessly. He was assured that eternity with Christ waited him on the other side.

Chapter Eighteen

A Son for Yun—Isaac

On April 19, 1984 Yun's wife, Deling, gave birth to a boy. Yun now had a son.

During her pregnancy, Deling had very little food to eat. Being pregnant and obviously showing, she still had to work many demanding hours out in the fields each day. During the first months of her pregnancy no one knew she was expecting. After Yun had been arrested and branded by the authorities as a criminal, many of her relatives and neighbors wanted nothing to do with her.

It is difficult for us in the west to understand that when a husband is imprisoned in China the family is left destitute, without any support whatsoever. The family have to endure severe poverty as all their belongings: pots, pans, furniture, and clothing are confiscated. Add to that the hostility from the neighbors and you can begin to understand the hardship faced. This is what Yun's family had to endure again and again, while he was in prison.

One night, just before the baby was born, Yun had a vision. He saw his wife coming towards him, proudly holding a baby in her arms saying, "Give a name to our son!" When he took the child in his arms he was reminded of a scripture about Abraham giving his son the name, Isaac.

Complications with Deling's pregnancy developed and resulted in her giving birth two months before her baby was due. On the evening of her delivery, the local government forced her to go to the hospital, intending to give her an abortion. With her mother-in-law and a few sisters-in-the-Lord present, they earnestly asked God for a miracle... and Isaac was born! The day after the birth, friends came to the prison and asked the guards to tell Yun the good news, that he had become a father to a son. One of the guards told him, "Yun, your wife gave birth to a child three days ago! Now they are going to celebrate this, and they have asked you to write his name on a piece of paper."

Yun got a pen and some paper and wrote the name, "Isaac," and then penned the following words to his baby boy. "When you were born your father was in jail for the sake of Jesus Christ. Daddy doesn't know if he will live to see you. Every parent wants his or her child to be somebody. But Daddy's only wish is that you will follow Jesus, and according to your name—Isaac—grow into a man of faith and obedience."

In the time that followed, it became easier for Yun in the prison. He was allowed to have more visitors who shared with him stories of the great revival going on outside the prison. They let him know that many people were being won for Christ as the revival fire burned brighter and brighter. Hearing this was such a relief and comfort to him!

However, the greatest joy he felt was in knowing that regardless of his circumstances and sufferings he had experienced the faithfulness of Jesus Christ. He knew that the Lord had a purpose for carrying him through the evil and destructive experiences he had been exposed to. His experience would be put to good use later in his life. Through these horrible, painful, and humiliating months he experienced what Paul wrote about nearly two thousand years ago:

"We are hard pressed on every side, but not crushed; perplexed, but not in despair; persecuted, but not abandoned; struck down, but not destroyed. We always carry around in our body the death of Jesus, so that the life of Jesus may also be revealed in our body. For we who are alive are always being given over to death for Jesus' sake, so that his life may be revealed in our mortal body." (2 Corinthians 4:8-11)

Chapter Nineteen

In Labour Camp— Then Free!

In October 1984 Yun was officially sentenced to four years imprisonment with hard labour. During his time in the labour camp he received very little food as he worked seven days a week, 14 hours a day.

One day the guards found a Bible in his cell, which of course was strictly forbidden. They immediately brought him into the interrogation room, where they beat and whipped him so hard that blood flowed. As a result he was sentenced to one hundred days in solitary confinement. This was really a solitary place, not much bigger than a broom closet. The room was about one meter high and one meter in width. He couldn't stand up and he couldn't lie down. It was damp and cold, and during his sentence he had to wear handcuffs the entire time.

For 10 days he prayed, asking God for a Bible. On the

tenth day a prison guard presented him with one. The prison officials had decided that Yun should have his 'religious freedom' while he was in solitary confinement and encouraged him to study the Bible!

Previously, no prisoner had ever been allowed to have a Bible or any other Christian literature. And now, strangely enough—they had given him permission to have a Bible, so that he could study it! God had not forgotten him, even if he felt buried alive in this little broom closet.

Upon his release in early 1988 the police lectured him on what he couldn't do once he was released. Familiar phrases that he had heard so many times before were once again repeated for his benefit. In his memory he could almost repeat them word for word. All house meetings were illegal... all preaching and evangelizing were strongly forbidden... and only the government-controlled church, the Three-Self Church was allowed. He was further warned, that if he and his workers breached any of these restrictions they would be arrested and harshly sentenced to prison.

To Yun, it was just as unthinkable to obey such an order now as it had been before. The Three-Self Church was still the same as it was before. It was not a church from a Biblical perspective. The government only created it to control the Christians, and promote their policies inside the churches. Further, it severely limited the ministry activities of its pastors and members. Of course, Yun and his people could not agree to this. Even though he and the other leaders do recognize that there are many good Christians at the grass roots level in the Three-Self Church, who are indeed committed and passionate for the sake of the Gospel—still, the facts do remain.

The top leaders of the Three-Self Church are in the hands of those loyal to the communist party. Several of them are very liberal theologians, who are barely interested in spreading even the social side of the Gospel. There are even some who are atheistic, as well as those who assert that the teachings of Christianity must adapt to socialism.

Yun was not intimidated by the warning and soon he was travelling, preaching, teaching and evangelizing as he had done before. His release from prison came at a very crucial time for China's house churches. God continued to use simple, uneducated people, to preach His Word and spread the Kingdom. There was no room for dry and highly learned theologians.

The fire of the Holy Spirit was spreading rapidly across many provinces. People everywhere observed many amazing supernatural happenings. Deaf people could hear, blind people could see again. Those who were sick and weak were brought to meetings, which at times numbered upwards of three thousand people. Yun and his co-workers laid their hands on the sick, and they were immediately healed. The power of the Gospel was the subject of conversation in the villages. The police were standing powerless, facing the power of God.

In June of 1989, the Tiananmen student movement was defeated. Thousands of young people who demanded freedom and democracy were arrested and killed. Up to this point the intellectuals were loyal and faithful disciples to the communist party. But now, many of them came to the conclusion that Marxism was empty and of no use. After the Tiananmen Square slaughter many intellectuals began finding their way to Christ.

Chapter Twenty

New Assignment: A Tool for Unity

During the 1990s Yun continued playing an important role in building the Church in China, despite repeated arrests, and a prison sentence.

Every time he was caught, he was exposed to severe mistreatment by the authorities. For nearly 20 years the government and PSB have been unable to break this man who is short in stature. Considered a danger to the entire communist system, Yun has been pursued as one of the most wanted criminals in China because of his leadership within the house churches.

In 1992, God gave Yun a new assignment that Yun didn't think he was ready for, and that he certainly wasn't expecting. In fact, he felt highly unqualified for the task set before him. God spoke to him, asking him to unify the different house church networks by finding like-minded leaders who shared the same vision.

When God spoke to Yun about this, he complained to God. Surely God could find someone else to accomplish this great task. Yun knew that the various house church movements inside China were suspicious of each other, not willing to trust. Creating unity among the different networks of house churches would not be an easy task and he dreaded it. For a long time the different leaders had talked negatively of each other and disagreed on several issues. To compound the problem, each house church movement looked at the other as a cult. Yun knew this and felt inadequate as he mumbled his response to God, much like Moses at the burning bush.

In the midst of Yun's moaning and grumbling session, God interrupted him by saying, "You are not My first choice." Now that God had Yun's undivided attention, He let him know that He had wanted many others to do it but that they were unwilling to obey Him. If Yun did not obey, God would look for someone else who would. This encounter changed Yun's attitude completely.

He began by going to the different leaders, and asked them to reconcile with each other. At that time, Yun made a covenant with the Lord, that he would not eat meat or eggs until unity had come to the house church leaders. One of the other leaders noticed this, and asked Yun why he was not eating. Yun explained why, and then the leader told Yun that he would do the same. Working diligently he contacted all the other house church leaders and they finally came together.

As the unity amongst them grew stronger and deeper, they came to a point where they could stand on the same platform. They started preaching in each other's churches, singing each other's songs and working together in different ways. Over time the mistrust disappeared, and unity took hold.

Later they agreed to call themselves—the Sinim Fellowship, after the words in Isaiah 49:12. "See, they will come from afar—some from the north, some from the west, some from the region of Aswan (Sinim)." Many scholars believe that the name 'Sinim,' is the same as China.

The leaders appointed Brother Yun as the chairman and spokesman for the different house churches of Sinim. At the beginning of the 21st century this community of Christians numbered over seventy million believers. Every day, 30,000 people in China turn to Christ as their Savior. That is nearly one million new believers each month—over 10 million new Christians every year! When the missionaries left China 50 years earlier, there were approximately 850,000 Protestant Christians in China.

What is so amazing, is that this tremendous growth in the church, is taking place in the world's largest communist and atheist state, which uses its influence to convince its people that God is dead! Twenty-five years ago, the western press stated that Christianity was dead in China. Mao's wife used to brag when facing foreign visitors, that the Christian faith would soon only be found in the museums.

Chapter Twenty-One

THE GATES OF IRON OPEN UP

This recently acquired unity amongst the house churches soon became a powerful force. The leaders started to plan how they could put this vision into practice.

In March 1997, the PSB police became aware that the house church leaders were meeting for what they called "unity talks." The communist party unfortunately, misunderstood the churches spiritual unity talks as being a political opposition party threatening the stability of the country. Fearful that these Christians would undermine the communist system, the PSB acted.

The house church leaders were meeting on the second floor of an apartment building, when without warning, the PSB moved in. Yun tried as usual to escape. He did this by jumping out of a second floor window. It was a long jump down, and he hurt both his feet in the fall. The police quickly arrested Yun and the other eight leaders.

Knowing Yun's history, the PSB officers sarcastically asked him if he would try to escape again. Yun responded, "If the Lord gives me an opportunity I will escape!" Angered by his answer, they took him up to the roof of a high rise building. A policeman pushed Yun towards the edge and told him that now was his opportunity to escape, "Go ahead and jump," he said with a grin.

But Yun answered that he would not escape this time, because the Lord had not told him to do so. The authorities were determined to finally break Yun for good. To insure that he would not escape from prison, they took a sledgehammer and smashed his legs just above his ankles. Only the flesh kept the bones together. It was impossible for Yun to either stand or walk. Once again he had to endure constant, excruciating suffering and pain.

The heavenly man was now a cripple, left to rot away in a prison cell, until the day he died. Then at last he would be set him free from his pain and suffering. This appeared to be his only prospect. At 39 years of age he would never again be reunited with his wife and family.

It became obvious that the other house church leaders would suffer for their 'crimes' as well. Once and for all, the PSB would put an end to the activities of these troublemaking Christians who would not respect the law. Everyone who was arrested was sent to a maximum-security prison that was well known as the best guarded and the most escape-proof prison in China.

A Christian Brother was ordered to carry Yun to and from the toilet and the interrogation room. Yun had already endured enough pain and suffering, yet they continued torturing him. They did everything they could to get information from him. Not only were they determined to lock him up for good, they were resolved to destroy him completely.

One day when he was in the bathroom, he had an opportunity to speak with one of the other Christian leaders. This Brother whispered to Yun, "You're the one to escape!" But Yun responded, "We are in prison. Look at my legs! I can't walk anymore. There are too many locked metal doors. How could I get out?"

A few days later, Yun met the same Brother, and again he repeated that Yun should escape. Yun reminded him that he couldn't walk and that the other Brother who was uninjured should be the one to escape.

Yet this Brother insisted, and kept repeating, "You can walk, you can escape!"

That same night, Yun could not sleep from the pain in his legs. He lay down with his back on the floor, and his legs up in the air, to ease the pain. All he could do was moan his despair to the Lord, "Oh, Lord! Once again I am in prison. My bones are destroyed. Now it seems that not even You are able to do anything. You called me to go to the west and to the south with the Gospel, but how can I do this now? I am laying here unable to walk. Am I a fool?" he cried to the Lord.

Once again, God was faithful to Yun and spoke to him these words; "This is the hour of your salvation." While still awake, he saw a vision of his wife, Deling, coming into his cell. She tenderly cared for his wounds.

Soon after this vision, he knocked on the door for permission to use the washroom. Again, he met the Brother who told Yun twice to escape. And for the third time he whispered to Yun, "Now is the time! Escape now!"

It was 8 a.m. on the morning of May 5th, 1997. This was the busiest time of the day in the prison and there were more guards on duty. Yun was brought back to his cell, and the door closed behind him. Yun decided this was the time for him to escape, even if it seemed totally impossible.

He took the first step in faith and obedience. The power of God went through him, he got up, HE COULD WALK! So he walked towards the door of his cell. The door opened!

He stepped out in faith into his freedom. Astonishingly, the doors kept opening up to him as he walked towards them! Many laws of nature were suspended. When he arrived at the main doorway leading to the prison yard, he saw another Christian Brother coming towards him. The door between them could only be opened by the prison guard pushing a button. Miraculously, as the Christian Brother came in through the doorway, Yun walked out, unseen. The Christian Brother, shocked at seeing Yun walking, said to him, "I am on my way in." Yun promptly answered, "I am on my way out."

Later, this Brother shared additional details about what happened, as seen from his point of view. "I was walking down the corridor after being examined by some prison guards. To my great surprise and fright, I saw Brother Yun. I knew he was crippled with his legs totally destroyed. Yet here he was coming towards me in a great hurry. Without hesitating he went straight out, through the gate! The prison guard who led me didn't see him at all. When I came back to my cell, I pulled myself up to the window, with its iron bars overlooking the yard. I could see Yun running across the yard, through the front gate, and out! There were probably 30 prison guards out there in the yard, but no one noticed the escape of Yun!"

Outside the prison, a taxi stood parked in the street. Yun walked up to the taxi, wearing his prison uniform, and got in. His uniform had no affect on the driver. He only commented about Yun being in such a hurry, and asked him where he wanted to go.

Yun remembered a Christian family who lived in this town, and he asked the driver to go to that address. When they arrived, Yun left the driver, and went in the house to ask for money to pay the driver. When he knocked on his friend's door they were too frightened to open it when they heard his voice. They asked if he had been released from the prison. He told them, "Our Father in Heaven asked me to come out from the prison, but now I need money to pay for the taxi." They gave him money and he went out to pay the driver. The cab driver looked at him in a strange way, not recognizing Yun at all! He just shook his head in disbelief, wondering why in the world a stranger would give him money?

He had no memory of Yun being his last passenger. God had wiped the driver's memory clean. The police would never get any information from him, no matter how hard they tried. Before his escape there were other unusual happenings taking place. Those who were involved testify as to the sovereignty of God in directing the entire escape.

The wife, in the home where he had escaped to, had fasted and prayed for Yun's release for over a week. Apparently, the Lord told her that he would soon be released, and he was going to visit their home first. She was also prompted to prepare a hiding place for Yun with food, clothes and a Bible.

Not long after he escaped from the prison, the alarm sounded. Once again the heavenly man, one of the most wanted men in China, had managed to breakout from an escape-proof prison to freedom. Much was at stake, both the prestige of the police and of the prison.

As Yun made his way to the safe house, a terrible rainstorm came over the city. Many stated that it was the worst storm ever to affect that area. Flooding led to a break down in the telecommunication system. Valuable minutes were lost to the police and the prison officials. But this was very valuable time for Yun! Before the security police had managed to put up roadblocks, he had been led to a secure place.

Many years before, God had told Yun these things would happen to him. God had been preparing Yun for this day through the Word of God and His Spirit. Thirteen years earlier, while Yun was in prison, God spoke to him saying, "The doors of iron will be opened to you, and you will be set free."

God had kept His word. When Yun walked through the first iron door, he was certain he was going to be discovered or worse still, shot. If captured, he was certain they would sentence him to ten additional years behind bars. But he acted in obedience. One iron door after another opened—and now—he was free!

Chapter Twenty-Two

ESCAPE OUT OF CHINA

Several days later, a pastor friend visited Yun in his safe house. As they walked, talked and prayed together they openly discussed what Yun should do next. "Where will God lead you now?" The pastor shared his conviction that God would give Yun the opportunity to take the message and the experiences of China's house churches to the rest of the world.

It's true that many miracles had happened in Yun's life, but how would he escape from China? From a human point of view, it seemed impossible that a man who was so wanted by the police would now be able to escape from the country. However, Yun's flight from the prison had also looked impossible to accomplish.

Yun remembered when he was a young boy, how God had told him he was going to be a prophet to many countries.

He asked Jesus, "Is this really the truth, or are You wanting to make a fool out of me?" But Jesus answered, "This is the truth. I have not changed."

So plane tickets were purchased for Yun on Lufthansa Airline's flight from Beijing to Germany. Yet, one major obstacle remained—Yun's passport. He had none! He had lost all his identification papers when he had been arrested years previously. To further complicate the situation, Yun was still one of the most wanted man in China at this time!

Surprisingly a passport was finally found for Yun. When he examined the passport to see what picture of his was in it, he discovered that it was not a picture of him at all, but a picture of another man with a different name! All he could do was pray and trust God.

When he arrived at the passport checkpoint at the airport, the officer stared at Yun and said, "This photo isn't of you!" Yun's response was simply to smile, for the Lord had told him not to say anything at all, just to be quiet. The officer once again examined the picture at the front of the passport knowing that it did not resemble the man standing in front of him. Yun continued to be silent, and looked innocently back at him—smiling.

Then the officer checked the computer register to find out if the police had a warrant for Yun's arrest. Of course, as much now, as before, he was one of the most wanted men in China. Pictures and information about him were certainly in all the computer archives, including the passport check in the airport. It was readily apparent that Yun would be arrested in just a moment's time and that he would be unable to leave China. But because it took so long to handle Yun's passport, many of the other passengers were growing impatient waiting in line to go through the passport control. The officer sensed the passengers' impatience, told Yun to step aside, and let the other passengers pass through.

After a while the officer came back to Yun and said, "Even if I let you go, you'll not get permission to enter Germany. You will be sent back again!" And with that he reached for his official stamp and placed the proper notification for Yun to leave the country. This comment showed he recognized that this smiling man in front of him did not have a legal passport. But why then, or how could he let Yun go? The answer to this is beyond reason.

At the gate where the passengers enter the plane, he had to show his passport and documents once again. The officer looked at Yun, and then at the passport. He made a call to check the documentation. Yun did not know what they were talking about, but he remained calm and smiled. He knew that as long as he was obedient and did what the Holy Spirit told him to do, there would be no problem. Finally, he passed through the checkpoint, and entered the airplane that brought him to Germany.

Hours later, he arrived in Germany, where he had to go through their passport control. The same thing happened. The officers looked quite serious when they looked at his passport. They examined the picture in the passport several times, looking back and forth from Yun to the picture.

It took a great deal of time, but finally they said okay and let him through! The Chinese passport officer was wrong! The heavenly man was not sent back. At last he could put his feet on European ground. Even if Europe was the center of materialism and selfishness, years ago, Europe had sent missionaries to his home country with the Gospel. Now he had come as a man, who throughout all these years had been living proof that what matters, is not rationalism and reason, but faith—and faith alone. He had taken care of what the missionaries had entrusted to his people.

Many months later, his wife and children also escaped out of China through miracles and wonders as well.

Chapter Twenty-Three

COMMUNISM CAN NEVER KILL THE DREAM

God told Yun, "In the same way that I brought you out from the prison, and out of China, I will take one hundred thousand missionaries out of the country, and send them across Asia."

After recovering in Germany from his escape and time in prison, Yun began his ministry to the west. One of the first countries he visited was Norway. Two times he came to Norway, and ministered, thanking the Norwegian church for sending so many missionaries to China. As he put it, they brought the "Light" to his people.

Visiting Norway was in many ways, Yun's opportunity to return to his spiritual roots. His mother had become a Christian through a Norwegian missionary. Though she drifted away from the Lord for a while, she returned and led her son to Christ. We remember the time when God called

Yun as a young man, to go to the west and then the south. It started in a few villages and gradually expanded from county to county, then from province to province, and now, all over China a mighty army stands ready.

Norwegian churches have a long tradition of sending missionaries out all over the world. When Yun shared his vision of sending out one hundred thousand missionaries, their hearts were excited. Their desire to partner with Yun in what God is doing in China has been overwhelming.

As the house church leaders met in January 2000, they established principles by which they will govern themselves in the twenty-first century. One of the principles established is "A commitment to emphasize evangelism and the fulfilling of the Great Commission through the power of the Holy Spirit."

When they are talking about, "Back to Jerusalem," it is important to understand that they have a goal in mind. First of all, it suggests the direction in which they shall go, to the west. This movement is not a race and neither is it to simply gather one hundred thousand Chinese missionaries in the capital of Israel for a conference!

On their way, there are many people-groups that will be reached with the Gospel, and churches will be planted. This will be a "mission journey," which will last for many years. No one knows how long it will take to reach the many people-groups as these missionaries journey towards Jerusalem.

The first of these missionaries are already on their way, and are situated outside the borders of China. Over thirty missionaries departed at the end of March 2000, and many more will follow. In the house churches there are more than one million pastors and evangelists. Of these, ten percent have a missionary calling on their lives. It is easy mathematics to figure out that one hundred thousand are willing to go!

Yun is the key person in this work, however he is not alone. The Chinese Christians emphasize what the Bible says about the Church—it is a Body. Each person has a different task and ministry to perform, yet are dependent upon each other if the Body is to function properly, as an army going into battle to win.

It's exciting to take a closer look at this vision of sending thousands of missionaries from China into Asia. One thing is certain, it is a vision shared by many that is neither new nor fanciful. Nearly half a century ago, before Yun was born, God planted this dream into many Chinese believers' hearts. They were looked upon as dreamers, but as far back as 1920 many of them began to gather in the northwest corner of China. Their goal was Jerusalem. However, they didn't get very far. They didn't even make it out of China.

These believers had read the Great Commission, and understood that God had called them to, "Therefore go and make disciples of all nations." They saw these words to Jesus' disciples for what they really were, a commission for ALL Christians, regardless of race and culture. It never entered their minds that the largest nation of the world, China, should be excluded from this task!

The Gospel puts everybody on an equal footing. Evangelizing is not only the white man's burden, even if many organizations in the west still act as if this is something they are especially appointed to do. In the '40s, a new generation took over the calling and the vision. Brother Yun met, at the end of the '80s, the old and highly respected pastor, Simon Tsao.

More than 40 years earlier, just before the communists took over, Simon Tsao and his wife started wandering to the west, towards Lanchow. Many followed them, and God gave them many songs about taking the gospel to the west. Interestingly, Simon Tsao wrote the songs Yun and the other Christians had been singing for many years. Brother Yun and his friends did not know this. One of these songs begins like this, "Lift your eyes to the west." Simon Tsao and the other wanderers came to the border of Xinjiang, in western China; there the communists arrested them.

Simon Tsao was imprisoned for nearly 40 years. The other Christians kept the vision warm during the difficult years that followed, when the persecution was severe. One of the songs they often sang ends with these words, "We have the same longing and the same wanting after the road to Zion. In the same footsteps we are marching on to Jerusalem. We have dedicated our hearts to the Lord—His power has conquered people of all nations. Oh, Lord Jesus Christ—who would not follow You?"

To them, the wandering towards Jerusalem had a symbolic suggestion. It meant a daily wandering with Jesus, and daily preaching of the Gospel. In light of these historic facts, we can make the point, that the calling to bring the Gospel first to China then all the way to Jerusalem, has been a living and powerful vision among the Chinese Christians for almost one hundred years.

After God had instructed Yun to seek unity among the house churches, Yun had his first meeting with Simon Tsao. The old man told him that his calling was especially to bring the Gospel to the Islamic nations, which were situated west of China. During their conversation, the elder, Brother Tsao, sensed that he was passing his mantle to a younger man who would succeed him. At last he met someone who was called to go to the west. He embraced Yun, and cried with joy.

The Cultural Revolution and the severe persecution that followed have not been able to kill the dream. It has now risen to the surface and into new young minds. It soon became clear that God was the one orchestrating the vision, since each house church movement received the same vision, independent of each other.

It started over 50 years ago in central China's Henan province. Since then it has moved farther on, like ripples in the water, flowing effortlessly to the west and to the south. China has experienced a tremendous evangelizing effort to millions of its citizens, including the many minority groups who are living inside the borders of China.

Many of these minorities have had a hostile attitude towards the Chinese. Moreover, the Chinese evangelists have supernaturally broken through these barriers. God has used their fearlessness and the Gospel's inherent power of creating reconciliation among people to penetrate these obstacles.

Those who are willing to throw away their prejudices against the Christian faith and look at it objectively, will soon discover that where the Gospel is given a chance to do its work, there will be reconciliation and peace—just as much among individuals, as among people-groups.

Looking at the '10/40' window—an area extending from West Africa to East Asia, from ten degrees north, to forty degrees north of the equator—you will find that nearly four billion people, over half of the world's population, is living in this area.

Both China and India, who together have more than two billion people, are situated in this strategic "window." Inside this area, 90% of the world's unevangelized people live. If the Great Commission is to be fulfilled, this geographic region in Asia must definitely be reached. In the Far Eastern country of China, God has raised up a strong and vibrant Church, called to reach the lost. It has been cleansed through much suffering. Now their hearts are burning with a passion to take the Gospel the last leg of the journey, before the return of Jesus Christ. To them, the mission fields are towards the west.

Chapter Twenty-Four

THREE ROADS—TO THE WEST AND THE SOUTH

The "Back to Jerusalem" movement has established three main routes in taking the Gospel through the final frontiers of the least evangelized nations in the world.

The first, is a northerly route that goes along the old highway between China and the Middle East—known as the Silk Road. It has been in use since before the birth of Christ. Marco Polo used these roads. It travels through the town of Kasgar in the west of Xinjiang, and through the central Asian republics in the former Soviet Union, Iran and towards the Mediterranean.

The middle road that is used is referred to as the Himalayan Road. It starts in Tibet, and will bring the missionaries via Bhutan and Nepal, towards Afghanistan, Pakistan, Iran and the Middle East and then to Israel. These two roads travel mainly through Muslim countries.

The third main road starts in Vietnam and goes first to the south and then to the west. In Vietnam, there are many house churches that have been started. The Chinese have close contact with them. If you continue westwards you come to countries like Cambodia, Laos, Thailand, Myanmar (Burma) and India. This route implies evangelizing right into the heart of the Buddhist and Hinduistic world.

None of these areas are secure or without risk to the travelling Christian missionaries. On the contrary, their presence will challenge the mighty spiritual powers and principalities. The Chinese missionaries know that many of them are going to suffer a martyr's death as they travel into nations that are strongly hostile towards the Gospel.

The first missionaries are already on their way. And many more are preparing themselves for the Great Task, and will soon follow the others. They are learning different languages, for example Arabic and English. They are also being educated in learning the manners and culture of the countries they will enter.

Chinese Christians have been evangelizing in the west of China, among the Muslims for some time now. Some Muslims have become Christians. Their Muslim background provides many benefits for entering Muslim areas further west. The Tibetan Buddhists are strongly against the Chinese, who have occupied their country. A number have accepted Christ, and are being trained to evangelize their fellow Tibetans.

In some neighboring countries there has already been significant revival, for example in Nepal, and in various parts of Vietnam and India. There are Churches in many areas, which can serve as a base for the further planting of Churches. The Chinese know that it is of no avail to come to these countries with words only. They must come in power as well, the power of the Gospel—with signs and wonders to convince the people that there is a living and real God whom they can serve.

Yun is a very influential person in organizing, training and sending out missionaries. Over the next five to ten years, more than ten thousand Chinese missionaries will have left China, going to the west.

Yun has been blessed with great authority and respect among the other top leaders in the Chinese house churches. He is an indisputable leader, whose views are sought after. Though having a major role to play, he stresses that everyone has their own assignment to fulfill and that without the leading by the Holy Spirit and a daily walk with Christ, their ministry will not succeed. There is a great, continued need for humility, prayer and the grace and wisdom of God.

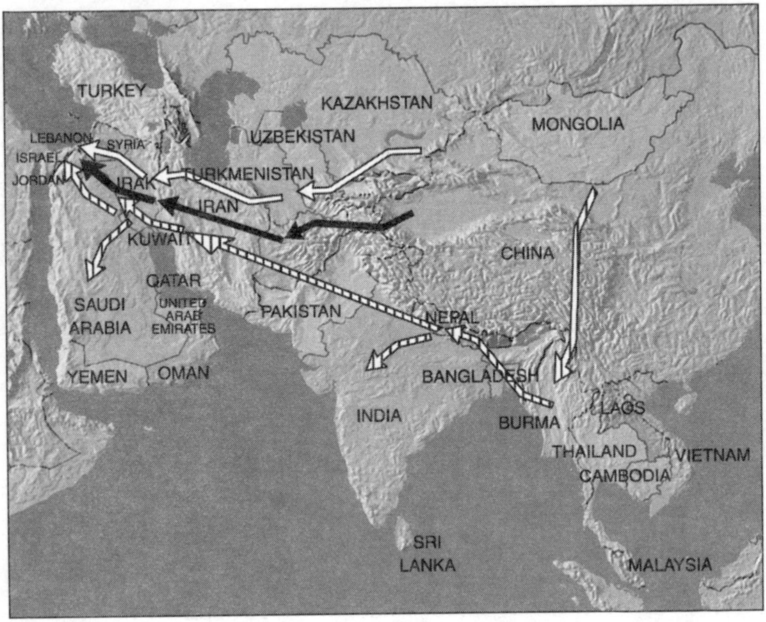

TURKEY
KAZAKHSTAN
MONGOLIA
LEBANON
SYRIA
UZBEKISTAN
ISRAEL
TURKMENISTAN
JORDAN
IRAK
IRAN
KUWAIT
CHINA
QATAR
SAUDI ARABIA
UNITED ARAB EMIRATES
PAKISTAN
NEPAL
YEMEN
OMAN
BANGLADESH
INDIA
BURMA
LAOS
THAILAND
VIETNAM
CAMBODIA
SRI LANKA
MALAYSIA

Chapter Twenty-Five

What About Us?

What part are we, who are living in the west, to play in this "Back to Jerusalem" vision? Should we have anything to do with this, and if so, what is our role? Perhaps it's best if we first clarified what it is we should NOT do.

Yun puts it quite succinctly. Whether it is practical ministries, teaching, Bible support, evangelizing, or the mission in general, everything needs to be under the terms of China's house churches. The Chinese know their country. They have an extraordinary knowledge of their own culture. They know how their society functions. And not the least, they know how the authorities are trying to gain control over Christian activities to destroy the house churches.

The Christians who are unregistered have traveled on a tremendously hard and difficult road of suffering. The cost has been huge in order to preserve the Church's freedom from the controlling religious system. For example, having the freedom to send out missionaries both inside and outside of China. The Three-Self Church have their hands and feet bound with regard to this task.

If the Churches in the west can understand and accept their role in supporting the Chinese Church, as it seeks to carry out the "Back to Jerusalem" vision, the Chinese Church is more than willing for us to participate. Yes, they are even praying for us to stand together with them. The "Back to Jerusalem" vision might well become a vehicle God uses to unify Christians from around the world into a more supportive and intimate relationship. In this way it can also serve as a conduit to an even deeper unity among all God's people in the western countries.

First and foremost, the Chinese Church wants us to stand together with them in prayer. Next, we in the west have the opportunity to use our financial resources to invest and support the "Back to Jerusalem" missions effort. It only takes approximately $100 Canadian to support a Chinese missionary and his family per month. There is also a need for funding to help in the training for these missionaries. The house churches are always eager to receive Christians from the west that can teach.

This book is primarily about Brother Yun, but we do hope that you as a reader have also gained insight into how the house churches operate. This is quite different from most churches here in the west. You would be perfectly justified in saying that China's Church looks very much like the Church we read about in the New Testament. They also have a clear understanding regarding the universal Church, and the interdependence and cooperation, that is a natural part of this Church. After all, we are all a part of the same

Body, regardless of race, nation, gender, age, or education.

The house churches DO want contact and cooperation. They welcome visitors, but in such a way that their security can be maintained. Brother Yun never tires of expressing China's gratitude for the western missionaries bringing the Gospel to them. Throughout the year, Chinese Christians will often visit the different locations inside China where some of these missionaries are buried and honor them with a memorial service. Again and again, Yun will tell you that as the missionaries suffered and died for the sake of the Gospel, the Chinese must be ready to do the same, to bring "Light" to the billions of people living in Asia's darkness.

In saying this, it is necessary to emphasize that they are not at all satisfied by the initiatives made by some western organizations. Unfortunately, projects are often started only because the organization or denomination has a need to draw attention to itself. This is not benefiting China's house churches! On the contrary, according to many house church leaders it often creates a lot of damage and frustration.

About Bibles

An example of not benefiting the house churches, is when western organizations raise funds for printing Bibles inside China, under the direction of the Three-Self Church. The organizations in the west will assert that the house churches receive their fair portion of these Bibles. What they are not aware of, is that the PSB police are in total control of the distribution of the Bibles. They keep a record of where the Bibles are distributed and who orders them. In this way, they can easily trace the house church Christians who are taking delivery of these Bibles.

Some Bible money even goes into supporting the TSPM church system. Sadly, at times those funds are used to control and suppress China's house churches. The house churches have decided that they will take care of the Bible printing themselves. If individuals or organizations from the west would like to contribute with financial support for Bibles for China, the house churches would gladly welcome such help, if it were handled through the proper channels.

ABOUT DENOMINATIONS

"There are many western churches, denominations and mission agencies which have their own agendas for China," Yun comments. Their intentions often depart from the house churches objective. Today a great deal of western churches and organizations give money to support the Christians in China, often with an ulterior motive that the Chinese churches will become 'branches' of the western denominations.

As a leader who has stressed unity, the heavenly man forcefully states, "We don't want western denominations and the discord that follows!" In saying this he means all denominations.

ABOUT BUILDINGS

The way the house churches organize and lead their churches is very similar to the times of the Apostles. They do not use their money to build and restore beautiful church buildings. They're not interested in spending money in this way.

In the west, building programs and church indebtedness is draining much of the Churches' resources. In January

2000, the Sinim leaders declared that, "We are committed to the model of the local house church without church buildings, in order to channel all the resources for the Gospel ministry and to bring honor to His Name."

They just follow what they have learned from the Bible, that buildings are useful in collecting people, but that is all. The Church is made up of Living Stones. It is Believers who make up the Body of Christ.

"Some of the western Christians would very much like to give their money to buildings, so they can have something specific to point at when they inform others about their investments. In this way they only are wanting to satisfy themselves," Yun claims.

The house church stresses, that it is not the number of people who gather in certain buildings on a Sunday, but how many are being sent out to evangelize that really matters! Europe is already full of great "empty" Cathedrals, where the need for a building was stressed. Within the next century, North America's great "church buildings" may also sit empty as well.

Additionally, if churches in China are going to gather their people in buildings, with a cross at the top of the roof, or on the wall, it will be much easier for the police to control their ministry. As we have seen earlier, Chinese law demands that the Church's activities are to take place at only one registered address. Ministry outside that address is frowned upon.

About Theological Education

Regarding the issue of persecution, the house churches have for many years remained silent on this issue. They have not wanted to draw attention to this matter because they have regarded persecution and suffering as something which God has allowed as an integral part in their sanctification. Everyone, who wants to follow Christ, will be persecuted. This was a "promise" Jesus gave His disciples. In this way, they will mature and be equipped in their ministry for the Lord.

Said as a joke, but with considerable underlying seriousness, the house churches have said that when theological issues are being raised, western pastors refer to different universities or bible schools. The Chinese on the other hand can only refer to the education they have gotten in prison, where humiliation, beatings, and other forms of torture are a part of their daily routine. "In the same way that we received our daily meal, this is also how we received the beatings," states Yun. "Fellow prisoners beat us and the prison guards beat us too. Yes, even officials, who were visiting the prisons, were allowed to amuse themselves with hitting us."

Because they feel that they are in debt to the Gospel, the torture, as they see it, is a way to pay that debt. But the house churches are no longer silent about the persecution and the oppression they have endured. In the latter years they have given the west a greater awareness of the conditions they are living under. It is now a normal practice to inform the west of the Christians who are imprisoned, and those who need intercessory prayer.

ABOUT HUMAN RIGHTS

Recently, the leaders in some house churches appealed in writing to the Chinese government, asking for acceptance and respect, but the authorities rejected their petition. The persecutions and harassment of Christians has continued with undiminished force. Actually, there have been more believers in prison in the last decade, than in the 1980s. Contrary to expectations, the pressure on the house churches is rapidly escalating, not decreasing.

The Chinese house church leaders feel comfortable about this being made known in the west. They are not pleading for human rights as a reason for any protest. The house church sees the west's heavy emphasis on human rights and democracy as taking the focus away from what is important. Doing so places man in the focus, and not God.

In many ways the Christians in China live in a vastly different world from those of us in the west. They do not want humanistic power to control the Church. In addition, they are critical of the west's passion for materialism, better living standards and new forms of entertainment that breeds a desire for experientialism. This form of self-worship will ultimately lead to emptiness, spiritual poverty, and to churches falling asleep at the wheel.

Yun states that the Chinese will come to Europe and North America to awaken "Churches which have been sleeping for a long time."

Chapter Twenty-Six

AND THE SICK SHALL BE HEALED

We started our story with a teenager in a small insignificant village, during China's Cultural Revolution. As a youth he received his calling as an evangelist to the west and to the south. He was obedient, never compromising, despite repeated imprisonment, persecution and suffering. Today, as a result, he has been appointed to lead greater ventures in the Kingdom of God. We can certainly see in Yun's life, God's faithfulness. What He promised, He fulfilled.

The 'gates of iron,' in a larger sense of the word, have opened up to him, one after the other. It was his mother who led Yun and the rest of his family to Christ. She is now over 80 years of age, still remaining a giant in prayer. Let us end with a story about this woman, who has played such an important role in her son's life, and in the life of the Chinese house church. Perhaps we can say that she has been one of the key figures in this huge revival, which has been going on for the last 20 years. In more than one way, the following testimony is representative of the supernatural power, as well as the miracles taking place in China's house churches today.

A few years ago, when she was in her early '70s, Yun's mother experienced a paralyzing stroke, losing consciousness. The doctors performed a variety of tests, indicating her condition was hopeless. According to them, she would never recover, and death seemed imminent. Her son was still in prison, unable to visit her. Yun's mother briefly regained consciousness, and asked her daughter-in-law to take her from the hospital to her home to die.

In a meeting of Believers who had gathered to pray for her in her home, God touched her. She was healed and began praising God. Now, she wanted to visit her son in prison. On her visit, she told him, if God had not healed her, he would not have seen her again, as the doctors had given up all hope.

A few years later, in September 1996, while he was preaching—Yun received a phone call stating his mother had again suffered a stroke. As a result she was partly paralyzed. The signs of the stroke were easily visible since her facial muscles were extremely contorted.

Arriving at the hospital, Yun came to her sick ward. His mother opened her eyes and said she wanted to be dressed in white clothes, as she was going to meet the Lord. During his visit, God spoke into Yun's heart that this illness would not lead to death. He fervently prayed over his mother with great authority, rebuking the illness in the name of Jesus. She felt such strength flow into her body that she got up, and walked! Her face was now totally normal.

Finally in the summer of 1998, his mother, for a third time became seriously ill. It happened after Yun had arrived in Europe. Everybody thought that she was going to die this time; her family had given up all hope. A coffin had even been purchased and delivered to her home. The family preparing for the end, dressed her in her burial clothes.

Her son, who had been so close to her over the years, was preaching in faraway Switzerland. When Yun received the news, he called her, using his mobile phone. Receiving his phone call, the family placed the phone close to her ear. Yun only uttered these words, "Mama, are you listening? Jesus loves you, and He will heal you!"

His mother—hearing the words, "Jesus loves you"—got up, moved around, and began to dance on the floor in triumph. Once again, God had given her victory over sickness and death.

The miracles following China's house churches are as many as the stars in the sky. We have only told a few of them. The greatest miracles of all are not the sick getting healed, but millions of sinners accepting Christ as their Savior and believing in the living God. In the days ahead, many will serve their Master along this road—towards the south and the west, throughout Asia—all the way to Jerusalem.

EPILOGUE

ASIA IS...

- The world's largest populated continent with more than 3 billion people (70% of the world's population).
- Experiencing unprecedented revivals and a sovereign move of the Holy Spirit.
- Challenging western Christians to become involved in reaching those countries that are totally or partly closed to traditional missionary efforts. It has the greatest number of unreached people groups who have never heard the Gospel message including the Muslims, Hindus, Buddhists and the Chinese.
- ...GREAT needs and many opportunities.

It was David Livingstone, the great pioneer missionary to Africa who said, "If I risk nothing, I shall gain nothing."

That is the true adventurous spirit touched by the living God.

ASIAN OUTREACH CANADA (asialink canada) is an interdenominational, evangelical and multi-racial fellowship of Christians serving God in Asia. For more than 30 years, our vision has been to partner together in mission so that the Great Commission might be fulfilled.

Unaffiliated with any organization of similar name, Asian Outreach Canada (asialink canada) is the Canadian partner of ASIALINK, a European mission society with indigenous organizations in Switzerland, Germany, Norway and Great Britain. All are working together in voluntary co-operation throughout Asia.

...OUR VISION...

- To evangelize Asia with the Gospel.
- To encourage national leadership in the development of indigenous churches in every Asian country.
- To be a "bridge builder" and a Christian link between the Asian Church and Christians residing in the western world.
- To maintain high standards of ethical integrity and to provide financial accountability with the finances entrusted to our care

OUR AREA OF MINISTRY...

Asian Outreach Canada (asialink canada) co-operates with local churches and organizations in China, Tibet, India, the Himalayas, Thailand, Sri Lanka, Bhutan, Pakistan, Bangladesh, Myanmar (Burma), Vietnam, Borneo and the Philippines.

- Church planting.
- Field training seminars for evangelists and pastors.
- Printing and distributing up to 100,000 Bibles monthly inside China.
- Providing humanitarian aid and assisting in the operational expenses of health clinics, schools, orphanages and child care centers.
- Underwriting the monthly support of needy children who have been rescued from destitute circumstances.
- Producing Bible teaching cassette tapes for distribution in the third world and videos for missions education.
- Underwriting the cost of Gospel radio broadcasts that are beamed into "closed countries."
- Providing Gospel literature for free distribution.
- Underwriting the purchase costs of bicycles to provide transportation for native missionaries inside China.
- Financially supporting evangelistic outreaches targeting unreached people groups in Asia.
- Providing emergency food and shelter for victims of natural disasters, wars and religious persecution.
- Co-ordinating short-term volunteers for cross-cultural and missions exposure in the areas of outreach, prayer, teaching English as a second language and medical missions.

Asian Outreach Canada (asialink canada) endeavors to partner with the national leadership in each country. They understand their own culture and are fluent in their own language. National leadership provides good management and stewardship with Christian accountability.

YOU CAN BE INVOLVED!...

P R A Y...

Asian Christians invite you to "pray for us." We believe for the evangelization of Asia and it begins with God's people "bombarding Heaven" with their prayers.

G I V E...

The monthly salary of the average Canadian worker equals the monthly support of up to 50 Christian co-workers in Asia.

Our monthly goal is to print 100,000 Bibles for distribution inside China.

We seek to keep administrative costs at a minimum. Government recognized donation receipts for income tax credit are issued to donors. Your dedicated stewardship is sincerely solicited.

G O...

Asian Outreach Canada (asialink canada) endeavors to mobilize and inspire concerned Christians to become involved in Asian missions. Canadian Ministry representatives would be honored to visit your local church, fellowship or Bible study group, to report on what God is doing in Asia. They will share the vision of what can be done to reach these special areas of the world with the Gospel.

Short-term volunteers are needed! Be a Bible courier, provide practical ministry with outreach evangelism teams. Health personnel for clinic and orphanage ministry are also desired.

YOU CAN MAKE A DIFFERENCE...

Western missionaries of yesteryear travelled to Asia and sowed the Gospel seed in believing faith. Many labored for years without witnessing any great response to their efforts.

Today, a tremendous spiritual harvest is being witnessed throughout Asia. Local Christians are taking on the central role in the evangelization and spiritual discipling of their countrymen. Asian Outreach Canada (asialink canada) is a resource centre to this ministry.

You are invited to become involved in "the greatest business on earth"—world evangelization.

Thank you for prayerfully considering investing in ministry that is changing lives.

CHINA Project 2000 and beyond

Is the goal of Asian Outreach Canada/asialink canada to assist the church in China, in the year 2000 & beyond, by providing Bibles, workers training cassettes, support of Chinese evangelists, and the first Sunday School curriculum to be published inside China in 50 years.

YOU CAN HELP CHINA

Bibles:

With China's Christian population numbering close to 100 million believers, the urgent need is still for Bibles. At present, these Christians have access to only 25 million Bibles. $3.00 covers the cost of printing a Bible inside China and delivery to the underground church.

Cassette Bible School:

The majority of China's 1 million pastors and workers will never have the opportunity of attending a Bible School. China's house church leadership have assumed the ownership of this project. This Bible School on tape, taught by house church leaders provides workers with the Biblical teaching they need! Each topic requires 15-30 tapes. $90 a year, or $7.50 a month, provides a Chinese worker with a tape recorder and study curriculum for one year.

Evangelists Support:

There are thousands of house church evangelists who require support for their families as they evangelize - keeping on the run, one step ahead of the police. As well, missionaries from China preparing to fulfill "The Back to Jerusalem" vision need monthly support for training. $100 monthly will support an evangelist and assist in covering their training.

China's First Sunday School Curriculum:

China has 400 million children under 15 years of age. How will they be reached for Christ? The house churches have prepared the first *inside China* Sunday School curriculum to be printed in 51 years of communist rule. This material is geared to sharing the Gospel with children who have never heard of Jesus. Your gift of $3.00 provides SS material for one child, $300 for 100. Help in the printing of this vital material!

Other Material Available:

Every Good Gift is an inspirational journey into the lives of Chinese Christians at a time when faith and commitment was as necessary to survival as physical nourishment.

Every Good Gift tells their stories - Bright Moon, Li Shan, Mei-Ling, and many others. Readers will learn much, about God's persistent reliability, about grace, and about China at a time where the faith of a few sent revival forward in the most uncertain times.

Read it! It will inspire you to face your circumstances knowing God can bring good out of anything."

- ✗ 32 Pages of never before published pictures of China's house church believers.
- ✗ Each story provides first hand accounts of God's faithfulness while enduring the fire of Communist persecution.

____Every Good Gift ($17.00) **$ ______**

____Shipping & Handling **$ 3.00** **Total $ ______**

China Prayer Map

Beautiful full color China Prayer Map showing the provinces and major cities in China that you can pray for. 33" x 23 1/2"

- ✗ Suggested donation $5.00 per map. Price includes shipping & handling.

____China Prayer Map ($5.00) **$ ____**

Please send order to:

Name____________________ Address____________________

City________________ Prov.________ Postal Code____________

☐ Please send me your free bi-monthly newsletter: **Impact Asia**

Make cheques payable to: *Asian Outreach Canada*

Box 939, Cambridge, ON, N1R 5X9

Phone: (519) 624 - 0223 ◆ Fax: (519) 624 - 0304
e-mail: aocan@golden.net

HELP US INVOLVE OTHERS

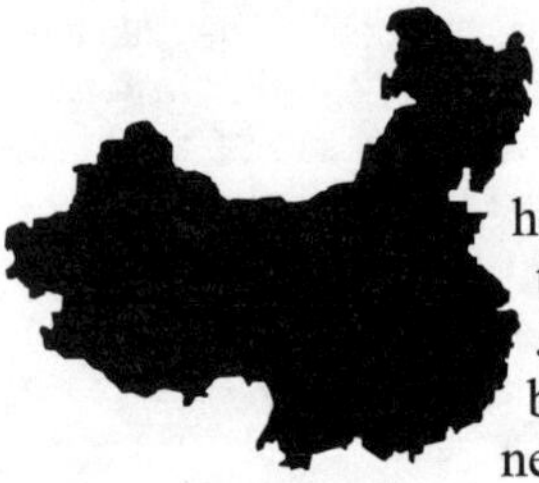

Give your Christian friends and relatives a FREE subscription to ***Impact Asia*** - to hear what God is doing in China and Asia today! Help give them a missions vision! Just fill out their names and addresses below. Use additional sheets of paper if necessary. **Please print clearly.**

Name______________________ Address________________________

City___________________ Prov._______ Postal Code_____________

Telephone (______) ____________ e-mail______________________

Name______________________ Address________________________

City___________________ Prov._______ Postal Code_____________

Telephone (______) ____________ e-mail______________________

Name______________________ Address________________________

City___________________ Prov._______ Postal Code_____________

Telephone (______) ____________ e-mail______________________

☐ Please identify me as the gift subscription donor. My name is:

X____________________________________

Please send your list of mission-minded friends to:

Asian Outreach Canada
Box 939, Cambridge, ON, N1R 5X9
Phone: (519) 624 - 0223 ◆ Fax: (519) 624 - 0304
e-mail: aocan@golden.net